C0-EDY-968

Critical Thinking about GEOGRAPHY

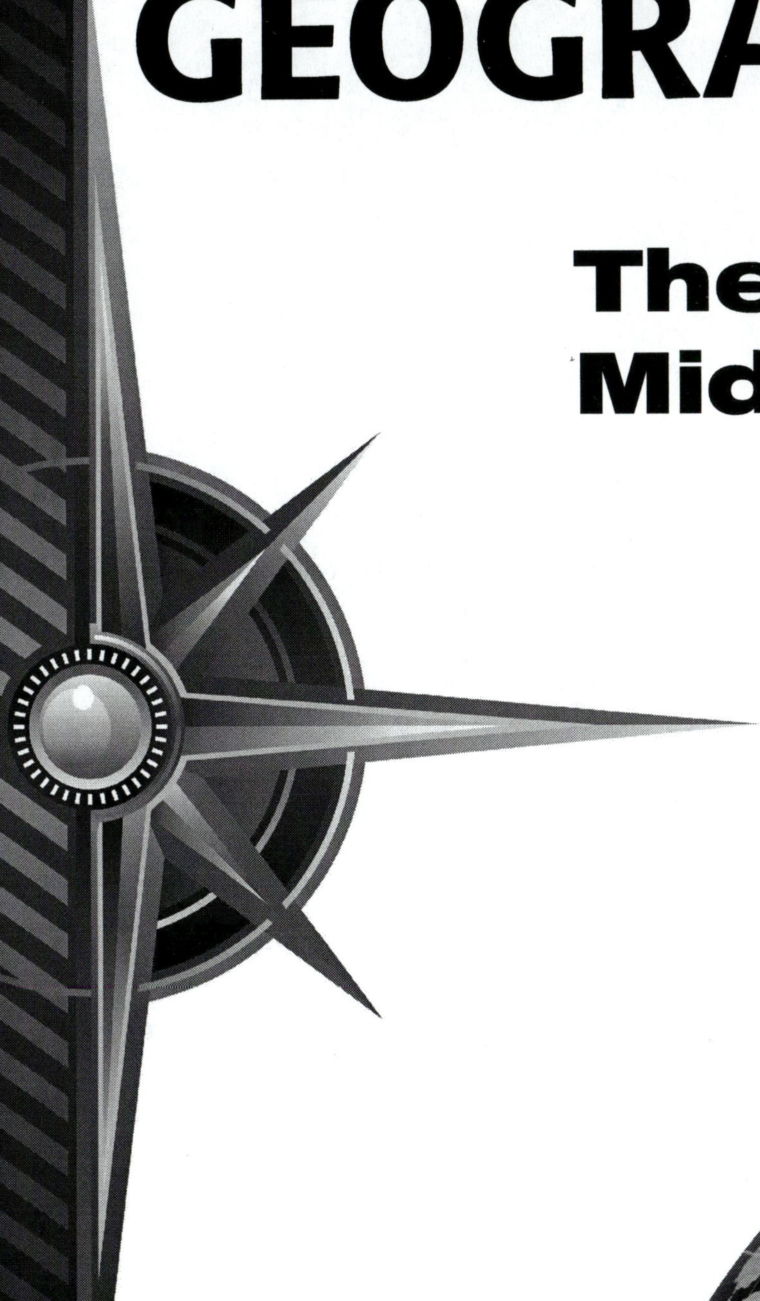

The Middle East

Jayne Freeman

WALCH EDUCATION®

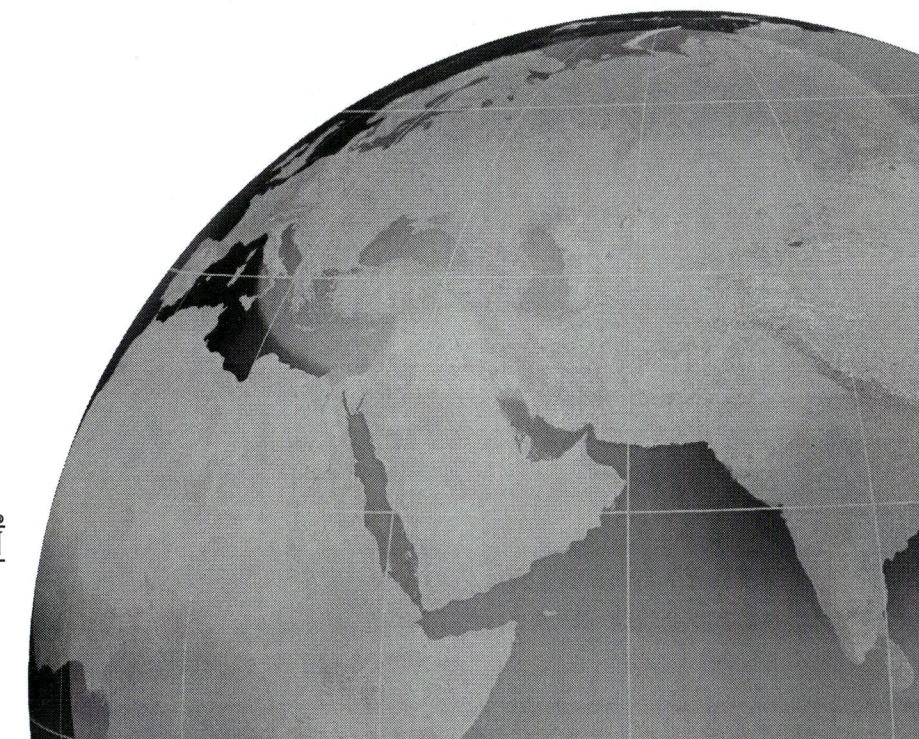

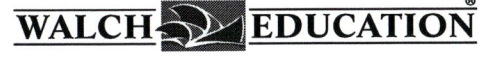

The classroom teacher may reproduce materials in this book for classroom use only. The reproduction of any part for an entire school or school system is strictly prohibited. No part of this publication may be transmitted, stored, or recorded in any form without written permission from the publisher.

SGS-SFI/COC-US09/5501

1 2 3 4 5 6 7 8 9 10

ISBN 978-0-8251-6596-2

Copyright © 2010

J. Weston Walch, Publisher

40 Walch Drive • Portland, ME 04103

www.walch.com

Printed in the United States of America

Contents

Introduction v
National Geography Standards vii

Lesson 1—Reading a Political Map 1
    Map: Political Map of the Middle East 4

Lesson 2—Using the Compass Rose to Read a Site Map 5
    Map: Site Map of Ibn Tulun Mosque 8

Lesson 3—Understanding Latitude and Longitude 9
    Map: World Map Showing Latitude and Longitude 12
    Map: Map of Saudi Arabia 13

Lesson 4—The Middle East in the World: Understanding Map Projections .. 14
    Map: Conical, Cylindrical, and Planar Projections/Mercator Projection ... 17
    Map: Peters Projection 18
    Map: Location of Mecca in Saudi Arabia 19
    Map: Lines of Equal Direction to Mecca/Map from Mecca 20

Lesson 5—Mountains and Valleys: Reading a Physical Map 21
    Map 9: Physical Map of the Middle East 24

Lesson 6—Exploring Economic Resources and Products 25
    Map: Economic Resources of Bahrain 28
    Map: Economic Resources of Iraq 29

Lesson 7—Reading a Land Usage Map 30
    Map: Land Usage Map of Yemen 33
    Map: Land Usage Map of Saudi Arabia 34

Lesson 8—Reading a Highway Map 35
    Map: Highway Map of Lebanon 38

Lesson 9—Understanding Population Density 39
    Map: Population Density Map of Yemen 42
    Map: Land Usage Map of Yemen 43

Lesson 10—Understanding the Importance of Petroleum in the Middle East 44
    Map: Middle East Production of Petroleum and Related Products (Natural Gas, Oil) 47

Lesson 11—Reading a Climate Map 48
    Map: Climate Maps of the Middle East in January and July 51

Lesson 12—Sources of Water in the Middle East 52
    Map: Mean Annual Precipitation in the Middle East 55
    Map: Sources of Water in the Middle East 56

Lesson 13—Coral Reef Ecosystems of the Middle East 57
    Map: Coral Reef Ecosystems of Middle Eastern Waters 60

Lesson 14—Comparing Historic and Modern Maps of the Middle East 61
    Map: The Middle East in 1860 64
    Map: Political Map of the Middle East (Contemporary) 65

Lesson 15—Boundary Disputes Among Middle Eastern Countries 66
    Map: Boundary Disputes in the Middle East 69

    Glossary 71

Introduction

Critical Thinking About Geography: The Middle East includes a collection of map activities that engage students in opportunities to practice and apply the geography skills and concepts that they are learning. It contains 22 maps with 15 accompanying lessons. Use these activities for whole class, small group, or individual instruction. A debriefing discussion after each map lesson provides an opportunity for students to reflect on their experiences and synthesize their thinking. It also provides an additional opportunity for informal assessment to assist instructional planning.

Implementation Guide

The following guidelines will help you prepare for and use the activity sets in this text.

Preparing for Instruction

Each lesson consists of instructional notes that provide background information about each map, answers to the student activity sheet, suggestions for debrief/discussion, and suggestions for extending and enhancing learning. Reproduce each map and have additional resources available to students. Prepare copies of student activity sheets (one copy per student in the class). Distribute any additional materials (if described in the instructional notes). To keep students engaged, have them record their answers on their own sheets of paper.

Timing the Activities

The activities are designed to take approximately 20 to 30 minutes per lesson. If time is short, you might plan to have students complete half of the activities in one session, and the rest of the activities on a different day. For longer periods, have students complete a group activity such as creating their own map. It is helpful to give students a "five-minute warning" before it is time to gather for a debrief discussion.

Debriefing the Activities

After students have completed the activities as a whole class, small groups, or individuals, bring them together for a brief discussion. At this time, you might have students pose any questions they had about the activities. Before responding to individuals, ask if other students encountered the same difficulty or if they have a response to the question. The class discussion is also a good time to draw out the essential ideas of the activities. The questions that are provided in the teacher's notes for each activity set can serve as a guide to initiating this type of discussion. You may want to collect the student activity sheets before beginning the class discussion. However, it can be beneficial to collect the sheets afterward so that students can refer to them during the discussion. This also gives students a chance to revisit and refine their work based on the debriefing session.

National Geography Standards

The geographically informed person knows and understands . . .

Essential Element I. THE WORLD IN SPATIAL TERMS

Standard 1. How to use maps and other geographic representations, tools, and technologies to acquire, process, and report information from a spatial perspective.

Standard 2. How to use mental maps to organize information about people, places, and environments in a spatial context.

Standard 3. How to analyze the spatial organization of people, places, and environments on Earth's surface.

Essential Element II. PLACES AND REGIONS

Standard 4. The physical and human characteristics of places.

Standard 5. That people create regions to interpret Earth's complexity.

Standard 6. How culture and experience influence people's perceptions of places and regions.

Essential Element III. PHYSICAL SYSTEMS

Standard 7. The physical processes that shape the patterns of Earth's surface.

Standard 8. The characteristics, distribution, and migration of human populations on Earth's surface.

Essential Element IV. HUMAN SYSTEMS

Standard 9. The characteristics and spatial distribution of ecosystems on Earth's surface.

Standard 10. The characteristics, distribution, and complexity of Earth's cultural mosaics.

Standard 11. The patterns and networks of economic interdependence on Earth's surface.

Standard 12. The processes, patterns, and functions of human settlement.

Standard 13. How the forces of cooperation and conflict among people influence the division and control of Earth's surface.

Standard 14. How human actions modify the physical environment.

Essential Element V. ENVIRONMENT AND SOCIETY

Standard 15. How physical systems affect human systems.

Standard 16. The changes that occur in the meaning, use, distribution, and importance of resources.

Essential Element VI. THE USES OF GEOGRAPHY

Standard 17. How to apply geography to interpret the past.

Standard 18. How to apply geography to interpret the present and plan for the future.

LESSON 1

Reading a Political Map

✦ **Goal:** To develop concepts and skills related to reading and understanding a political map

National Geography Standards

Standard 1. How to use maps and other geographic representations, tools, and technologies to acquire, process, and report information from a spatial perspective.

Preparing Students for Instruction

Before starting this activity, review the following with students:

+ Make sure students understand how to read a map legend.
+ Review measuring distance using a map scale.
+ Review the names and locations of continents on our planet.

Map Overview

This map shows the location of the group of countries generally referred to as the Middle East. These countries are at the point where three continents meet—Asia, Africa, and Europe. Technically, the Middle East is in Asia, but some countries straddle the continental boundaries.

Answer Key
1. Any four of the following: Turkey, Syria, Iran, Jordan, Saudi Arabia, and Kuwait
2. Africa, Europe, and Asia
3. Any four of the following: Black Sea, Caspian Sea, Mediterranean Sea, Arabian Sea, Aral Sea, Red Sea, and Sea of Azov
4. Turkey
5. Answers will vary. Based on the water that surrounds much of the land, students may infer that shipping and fishing would be common industries. Be sure that student responses are justified by information shown on the map, and not on other information they may bring to this question. For example, students may be aware of oil reserves in the area. The map, however, does not show this information.
6. Answers will vary. Students may postulate that differences in language, customs, type of government, or religion may have caused the establishment of these countries.

© 2010 Walch Education

Discussion Guide

To support students in reflecting on the activities and to gather some formative information about student learning, use the following prompts to facilitate a class discussion to "debrief" the map activities.

Prompts/Questions

1. Which countries on the map have you heard of? What do you know about them?
2. How might the existence of seas encourage settlement in the Middle East?

Suggested Appropriate Responses

1. Answers will vary but may include Turkey, Afghanistan, Iraq, Israel, and Iran.
2. Answers will vary. Students may postulate that the first settlers in this area may have arrived by ship. The opportunity to use the oceans and seas as highways to export and import goods may also have encouraged settlement.

Extending and Enhancing Learning

- Assign students to work individually or in pairs to investigate different countries in the Middle East. Have them find out about language, dress, customs, food, religion, interesting historical events, housing, architecture, and so on. After students have completed the research, have each individual or pair introduce the country to the class. Display a large map of the Middle East so student presenters can point to the country they are "introducing."

- For students who need more support, have them play a "Who Am I?" game to locate Middle East countries on the map. Draw up a set of clues such as "I am a country south of the United Arab Emirates. My coastline borders the Gulf of Aden and the Red Sea. Who am I?" Students will then locate Yemen on the map. They may write down the country names after finding them, or they may identify them to a partner. Have partners make up the questions themselves.

- To challenge students further, have them find out about the many bodies of water in this area and how they are used by these countries. How crucial to sea traffic is the Suez Canal, for example, or what historic biblical story involved the Red Sea?

Name: _____

 **LESSON 1** # Reading a Political Map

Geography Vocabulary

equator: a line of latitude that circles the earth and divides it evenly in half

political map: a map showing countries in a region, or a single country's territories, states or provinces, boundaries, and capitals

Tropic of Cancer: a line of latitude about 23 degrees north of the equator

Reading the Map

Many countries make up the region called the Middle East. Some of them are very small. Others, such as Iran, are large. Study the map. Think about what might have caused people in this area to form small nations. Did they begin as larger entities and then divide into smaller groups? Have they always been the same countries that they are now?

Understanding the Map

1. Name four countries that have a boundary with Iraq.
2. The Middle East is located at a point at which three continents come together. Name those continents.
3. Name at least four bodies of water shown on the map with "Sea" as part of their names.
4. What country is just north of Syria?

Analyzing the Map

5. Looking at the map, what industries would you expect to find in the Middle East? Explain.
6. Some countries in the Middle East are very small. Why do you think that is? Explain.

© 2010 Walch Education   Critical Thinking About Geography: The Middle East   **3**

Name: _____

LESSON 2
Using the Compass Rose to Read a Site Map

**Goal:** To develop concepts and skills related to reading a site map of a relatively small area using the map's legend and compass rose

National Geography Standards

Standard 1. How to use maps and other geographic representations, tools, and technologies to acquire, process, and report information from a spatial perspective.

Preparing Students for Instruction

Before starting this activity, review the skills of using a legend and a compass rose.

Map Overview

Over 90 percent of the population of the Middle East are Muslim people who subscribe to the religion of Islam. A building used for public worship by Muslims is called a mosque. This diagram shows the interior of a mosque. Point out the special areas inside the mosque to students as they examine the map. Explain that Muslims face Mecca, their holy city, when they pray. The founder of their religion, Mohammed, was born there.

Answer Key
1. Upper right
2. Southeast
3. About 77 yards
4. About 215 yards
5. The prayer hall
6. The audience will already be facing the prayer leader, because the mihrab directs them to face in its direction.

© 2010 Walch Education · Critical Thinking About Geography: The Middle East · 5

Discussion Guide

To support students in reflecting on the activities and to gather some formative information about student learning, use the following prompts to facilitate a class discussion to "debrief" the map activities.

Prompts/Questions

1. How would this map help someone who had never been to the mosque and wanted to worship there?
2. There are other areas in the mosque besides the prayer hall. How do you suppose the forecourt and the main court are used?

Suggested Appropriate Responses

1. The map would help a worshipper find the prayer hall, and show the worshipper which direction to face when praying.
2. Answers will vary. Students may suggest that they serve as quiet walking areas for meditation. The main court might be used for gatherings other than prayer.

Extending and Enhancing Learning

- Have students work in pairs or small groups to make a site map of a local gathering place such as their school, their neighborhood, a mall, or a supermarket. Have them include a compass rose and an (estimated) map scale, and create a legend that includes symbols for important items on the map. Completed maps can be displayed in class.

- For students who need more support, have them work more with the map scale and the compass rose. Using the map scale, they can measure distances on the mosque map. Using the compass rose, they can decide which way they would be facing in different parts of the mosque.

- To challenge students further, have them research the city of Mecca and its history, then write a report that includes a map of the city and an explanation of the reason why Muslims make pilgrimages to this city.

Name: _____

LESSON 2
Using the Compass Rose to Read a Site Map

Geography Vocabulary

compass rose: an element of a map used to show direction

site map: a detailed map of a relatively small area

✦ Reading the Map

This map shows the interior of a building used for public worship by Muslims. It is called a mosque. Most mosques share certain features. One is the minaret. This is a tower from which a call to prayer is issued four times a day by a man called a "muezzin." Find the minaret on this map. Next, find the minbar and mihrab. Read what functions they have in the mosque.

✦ Understanding the Map

1. Look at the compass rose. Normally the compass rose on a map is oriented with north at the top of the map. If you entered this mosque and faced north, which part of the map would you be facing: the top, upper left, upper right, side, lower left, or lower right?

2. Find the mihrab on this map. When Muslims pray, they always face their holy city, Mecca. Mecca is where Mohammed, the founder of this religion, was born. The mihrab is a place in the mosque that directs worshippers toward Mecca. In which compass direction would you be facing if you were looking at the mihrab in this mosque? Use the compass rose to help you.

3. Use the map scale. Measure the width of the main court in yards. Give a close approximation.

4. Imagine this: You walk in the entrance of the mosque. You walk down the forecourt to its end. Turn left. Walk to the minaret. About how many yards have you walked?

✦ Analyzing the Map

5. In which area of the map do most people probably gather when the call to prayer sounds from the minaret?

6. Why do you think the minbar is usually located next to the mihrab? Explain.

© 2010 Walch Education   Critical Thinking About Geography: The Middle East   **7**

Name: _____

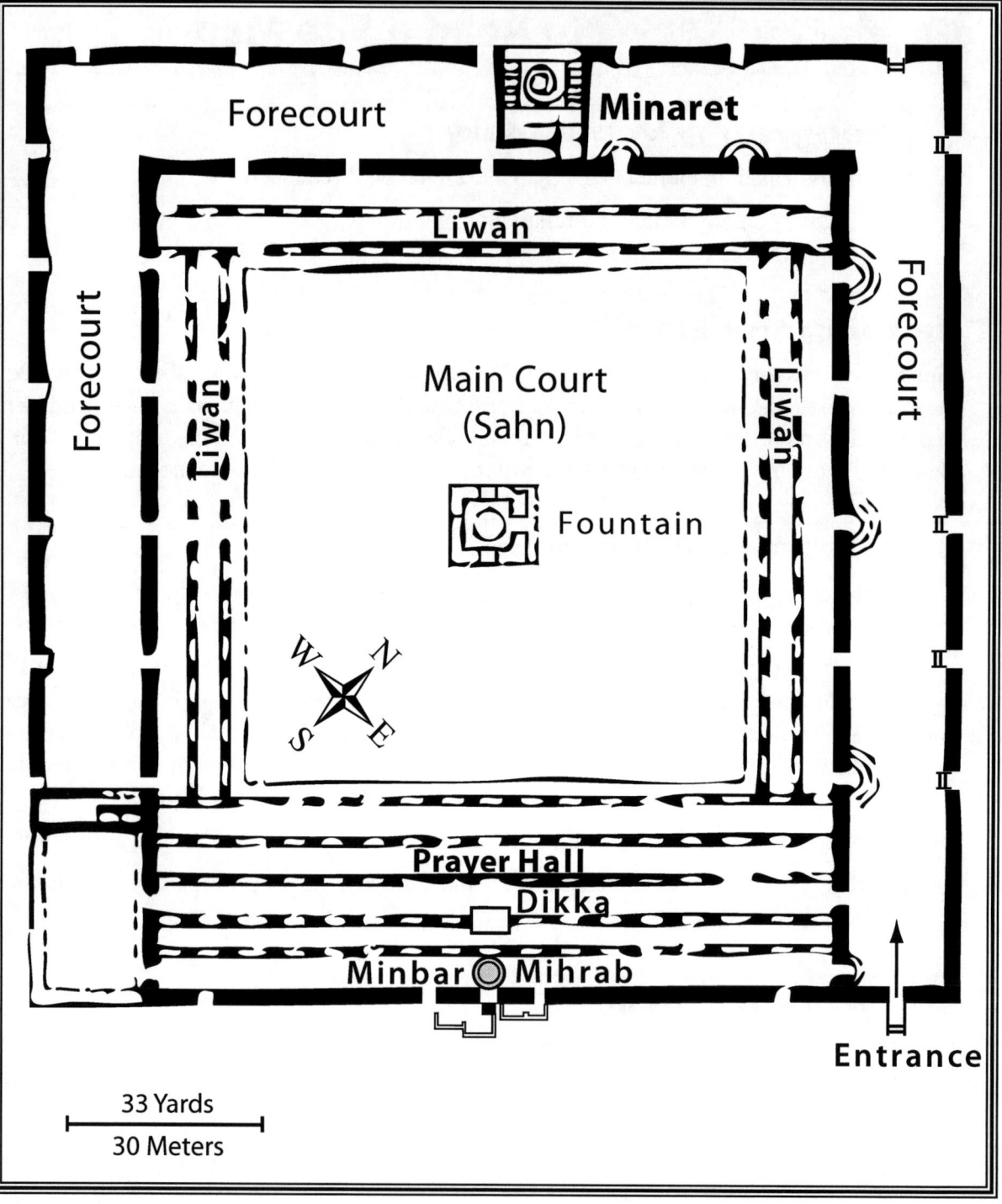

The mihrab is a niche in a wall of a mosque that is closest to Mecca. It shows the direction people should face when praying. Muslims pray facing Mecca. The minbar is usually to the right of the mihrab when a person is facing it. The minbar is a pulpit from which a sermon would be delivered. It looks like a domed box with a door at the top of a staircase.

 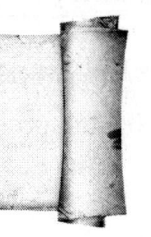

LESSON 3: Understanding Latitude and Longitude

Goal: To develop concepts and skills related to latitude and longitude and their uses to locate places on a map and in the real world

National Geography Standards

Standard 1. How to use maps and other geographic representations, tools, and technologies to acquire, process, and report information from a spatial perspective.

Preparing Students for Instruction

Before starting this activity, review the following with students:

- latitude
- longitude
- equator
- prime meridian

Map Overview

Students will examine maps of the world and of Saudi Arabia that show latitude and longitude lines. They will use map coordinates to find specific locations.

Answer Key
1. East
2. Saudi Arabia, United Arab Emirates, and Oman
3. Al Madinah and Riyadh
4. About 25 degrees north and 47 degrees east
5. The Red Sea and the Persian Gulf
6. Access to the sea provides opportunity for importing and exporting goods. It means business and sources of needed items such as food.

Discussion Guide

To support students in reflecting on the activities and to gather some formative information about student learning, use the following prompts to facilitate a class discussion to "debrief" the map activities.

Prompts/Questions

1. Why do you think that mapmakers divided the world into grids by using the system of latitude and longitude?
2. In what sort of career or business would latitude and longitude be important?
3. A device called a Global Positioning System uses information from satellites to inform people of their exact locations and give precise directions to destinations. Many cars have these devices, and handheld versions also exist. How would you use a GPS if you had one?

Suggested Appropriate Responses

1. It is easier to locate a specific place if your destination has coordinates based on this system.
2. Answers will vary, but students may say that any kind of travel or transportation can benefit from latitude and longitude. Ships at sea, planes in the air, and people traveling on the ground can all find where they are going.
3. Answers will vary but may include traveling by car or on foot to somewhere one has never been before.

Extending and Enhancing Learning

- Have students work in small groups to play a "Where Am I?" game. Create a set of about 20 cards with latitude, longitude, and a brief description on one side, and the name of a city or country on the other. Each player draws a card, reads the information on it, and uses the maps in this lesson to find the answer. After the player has stated an answer, the card is turned over to verify it. Players earn points for correct answers and play until you call "time." A sample card might read like this: "I am a body of water. I am at latitude 24° north and longitude 36° east." On the other side, the card reads "The Red Sea."

- For students who need more support, give them the latitudes and longitudes of places in Saudi Arabia, and have them locate each place. Then have them reverse this activity. They find a city on the map and give its latitude and longitude.

- Ankara, Turkey, and Philadelphia, Pennsylvania, share nearly the same latitude. Sana'a, Yemen, is at nearly the same latitude as the city of Brasilia in Brazil. Have students research the similarities and differences in climate and season in these cities, or other such "latitude pairs."

Name: _____

LESSON 3
Understanding Latitude and Longitude

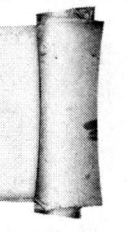

Geography Vocabulary

equator: a line of latitude that circles the earth and divides it evenly in half

latitude: imaginary circles on the earth's surface, parallel to the equator and above and below it

longitude: imaginary lines on the earth's surface passing through the North and South poles

meridian: a line of longitude; an imaginary great circle on the earth's surface passing through the North and South poles

parallels: lines of latitude; imaginary circles on the earth's surface, parallel to the equator and above and below it

prime meridian: the line of longitude numbered zero

Tropic of Cancer: a line of latitude about 23 degrees north of the equator

Tropic of Capricorn: a line of latitude about 23 degrees south of the equator

✦ Reading the World Map

This world map shows lines of latitude and longitude. Lines of latitude run parallel to the equator. These lines are numbered north and south of the equator. The equator is the zero line. On this map, the equator is a heavy dark line. Lines of longitude run north and south through the poles. These lines are numbered east and west of the zero meridian. The zero meridian is called the prime meridian. It is also a heavy dark line on this map.

✦ Reading the Map of Saudi Arabia

Locate Saudi Arabia on both maps. Look for the distinctive shape of the land it occupies. The countries just below it are Yemen and Oman. Saudi Arabia is part of a large peninsula.

✦ Understanding the Maps

1. Find the prime meridian on the world map. Is the Middle East west or east of the prime meridian?

2. Look at the map of Saudi Arabia. Through which countries in the Middle East does the Tropic of Cancer run?

3. Look at the map of Saudi Arabia. Which two cities lie on or very close to the parallel that is 24 degrees north of the equator?

4. Estimate the latitude and longitude of the capital city of Saudi Arabia. State whether the latitude is north or south of the equator, and whether the longitude is east or west of the prime meridian.

✦ Analyzing the Maps

5. Which two major bodies of water border Saudi Arabia?

6. How does access to these bodies of water help the country of Saudi Arabia?

© 2010 Walch Education   Critical Thinking About Geography: The Middle East   **11**

Name: _____

World Map Showing Latitude and Longitude

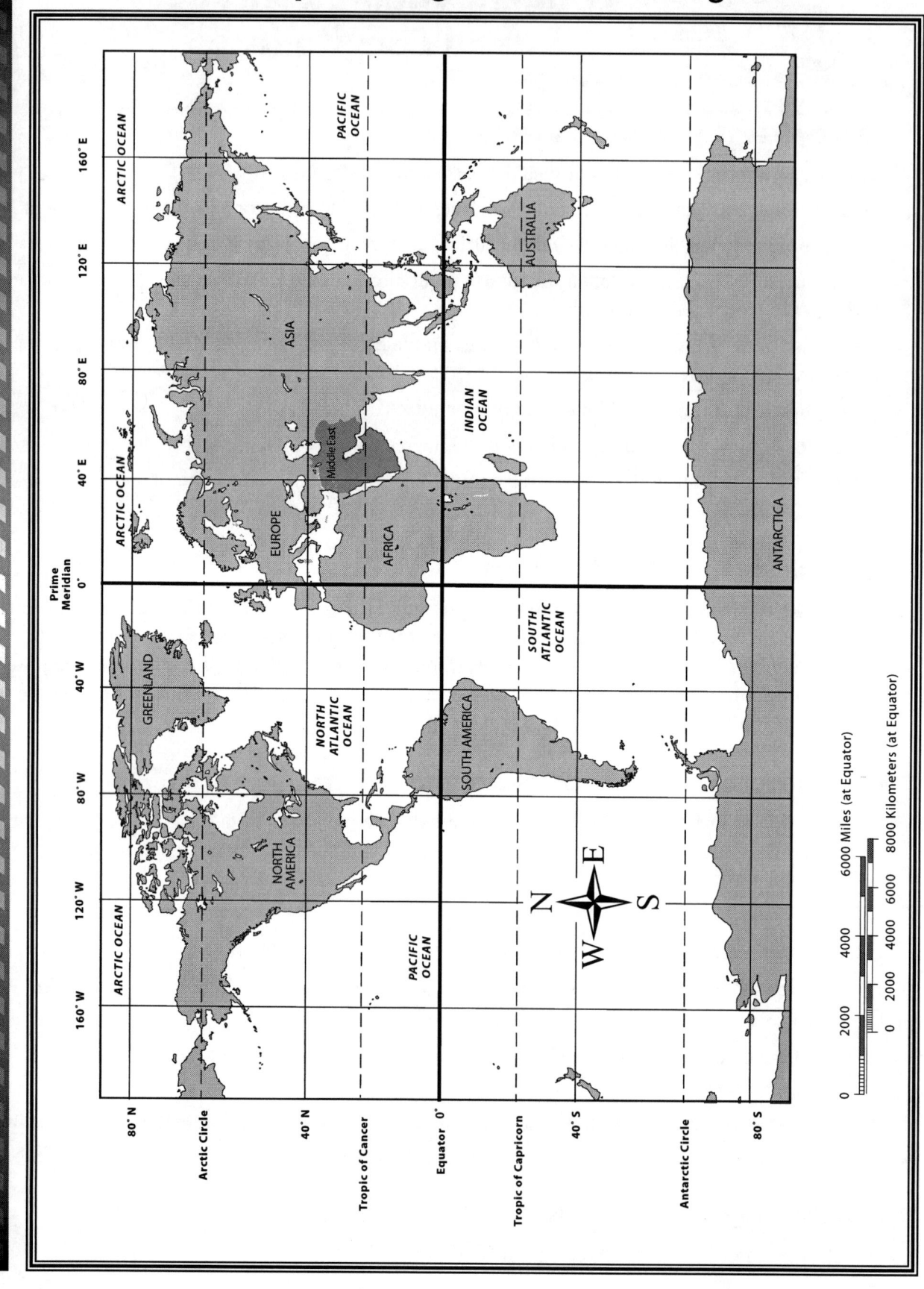

12 *Critical Thinking About Geography: The Middle East* © 2010 Walch Education

Name: _____

Map of Saudi Arabia

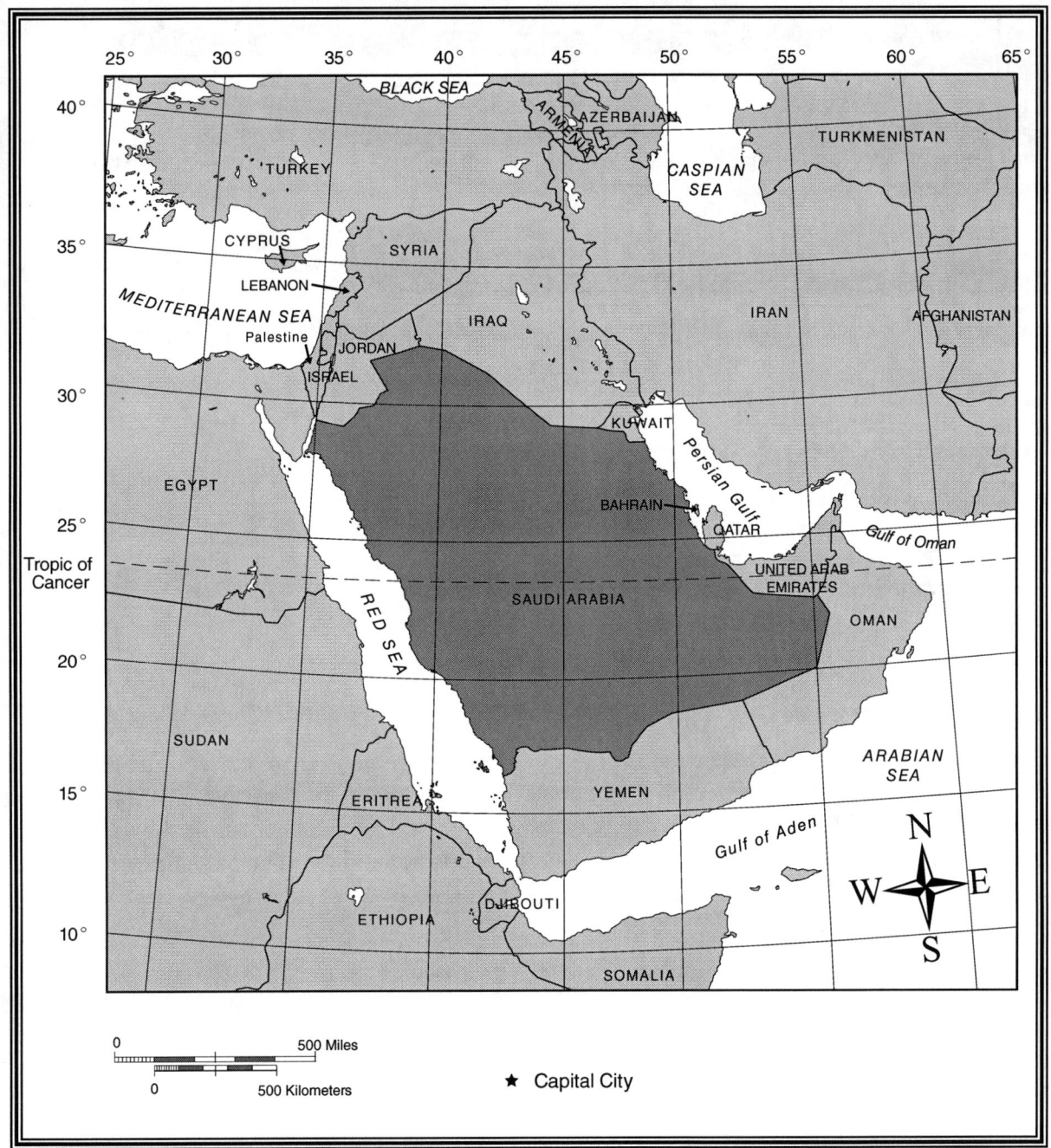

© 2010 Walch Education   Critical Thinking About Geography: The Middle East   13

LESSON 4

The Middle East in the World: Understanding Map Projections

Goal: To develop concepts and skills related to an awareness of different kinds of map projections and their uses

National Geography Standards

Standard 1. How to use maps and other geographic representations, tools, and technologies to acquire, process, and report information from a spatial perspective.

Preparing Students for Instruction

Before starting the first activity, review the following with students:

- equator
- lines of latitude
- lines of longitude

Map Overview

Because all maps are flat representations of a round planet, all maps are distorted. The amount of distortion varies among different map projections. There are many different types of map projections, but all have some kind of inaccuracy. The Mercator projection is widely used for ship navigation because its straight lines correspond to the great circle lines of a globe. The planar projection accurately depicts the poles. A conical projection will be most accurate in the area where the cone touches the globe.

Answer Key
1. The Peters projection
2. The planar projection, because it is most accurate where it touches the globe, and this projection can be made touching the South Pole.
3. The city of Mecca
4. Answers may vary, but students should notice that on the map going from Mecca, lines of longitude all converge on Mecca. Lines of latitude and longitude form increasingly large rectangles as they move away from Mecca. On the map going to Mecca, there are two sets of curving lines beginning at the sides of the map and ending at Mecca.
5. South along the center vertical line
6. Africa
7. Yes, because drawing a straight line from Mecca to central South America leads through Africa.

14 Critical Thinking About Geography: The Middle East   © 2010 Walch Education

Discussion Guide

To support students in reflecting on the activities and to gather some formative information about student learning, use the following prompts to facilitate a class discussion to "debrief" the map activities.

Prompts/Questions

1. Compare the Mercator and Peters projections. Look at large land masses. Which ones are obviously distorted either in shape or in size?
2. If you were traveling from the lower tip of India to Yemen, would you want to plan your trip using the Mercator or the Peters projection? Why?
3. What did you learn about mapmaking from the activity with the balloon? (See Extending and Enhancing Learning section below.)

Suggested Appropriate Responses

1. Answers may vary, but shape and size are very different on each map.
2. The Mercator, because lines of latitude and longitude are accurate on this map
3. Awareness of the difficulty of trying to portray a round object on a flat surface

Extending and Enhancing Learning

- Have students make a model globe by blowing up a round balloon, tying it carefully, and covering it with strips of papier mâché. After the papier mâché has dried, students can paint the continents on the globe. Then have them cut equal portions of the globe into strips in order to make it flat. Observe the distortion that occurs.

- For students who need more support, have them compare each continent displayed on the Mercator and Peters projections with the same continent on a globe, and decide what, if any, differences there are. Remember that the globe will always show the most accurate size, shape, and location.

- To challenge students further, have them examine the Mollweide, Eckert, Robinson, and Sinusoidal projections and explain their differences and utility either in a written report or by creating a chart.

Name: _____

LESSON 4
The Middle East in the World: Understanding Map Projections

> **Geography Vocabulary**
>
> **continents:** the major land masses on Earth
>
> **distortion:** a change in the shape of an image resulting from imperfections in portraying it
>
> **map projections:** attempts to portray the surface of the earth or a portion of the earth on a flat surface

 ## Reading the Maps

The illustration on top of the next page shows three ways of making a map by projecting a light through a globe onto a flat surface. Maps are two-dimensional portrayals of our three-dimensional planet. Maps are flat and the earth is a globe. No map can show an area on our planet as accurately as a globe. Some maps distort the shape or size of the land masses. Others distort distances.

Now find the Middle East on the Mercator projection map and the Peters projection map.

Look at the maps showing routes to and from Mecca. To Muslims, Mecca is a holy city. Every Muslim is supposed to make a journey to Mecca at least once in his or her lifetime. As a result, maps of the world showing routes to and from Mecca were created. The lines on the map <u>to</u> Mecca show the shortest routes to Mecca using a Mercator projection. The map of routes <u>from</u> Mecca, which uses an equidistant projection, are different from the routes <u>to</u> Mecca. You would find the shortest route home from Mecca by drawing a straight line from Mecca to your destination.

 ## Understanding the Maps

1. On which world map projection does the Middle East seem larger? (*Hint:* Compare to another land mass such as Australia on each map.)

2. Which type of projection would you want if you were going to explore Antarctica? Why?

3. Look closely at the map showing routes <u>from</u> Mecca. Most world maps are centered on the equator or some large land mass. Where is this map centered? (*Hint:* Consider its purpose.)

 ## Analyzing the Maps

4. How are the maps of routes to and from Mecca different?

5. Imagine your home was in Somalia. Along what lines and in what direction would you travel if you were going home from Mecca?

6. Imagine you were traveling to Mecca from the middle of South America using the map showing routes <u>from</u> Mecca. What continent would you cross before you arrived in Mecca?

7. If you returned from Mecca to central South America using the map of routes <u>to</u> Mecca, would you cross that same continent on your way home? Explain.

16 Critical Thinking About Geography: The Middle East   © 2010 Walch Education

Name: _____

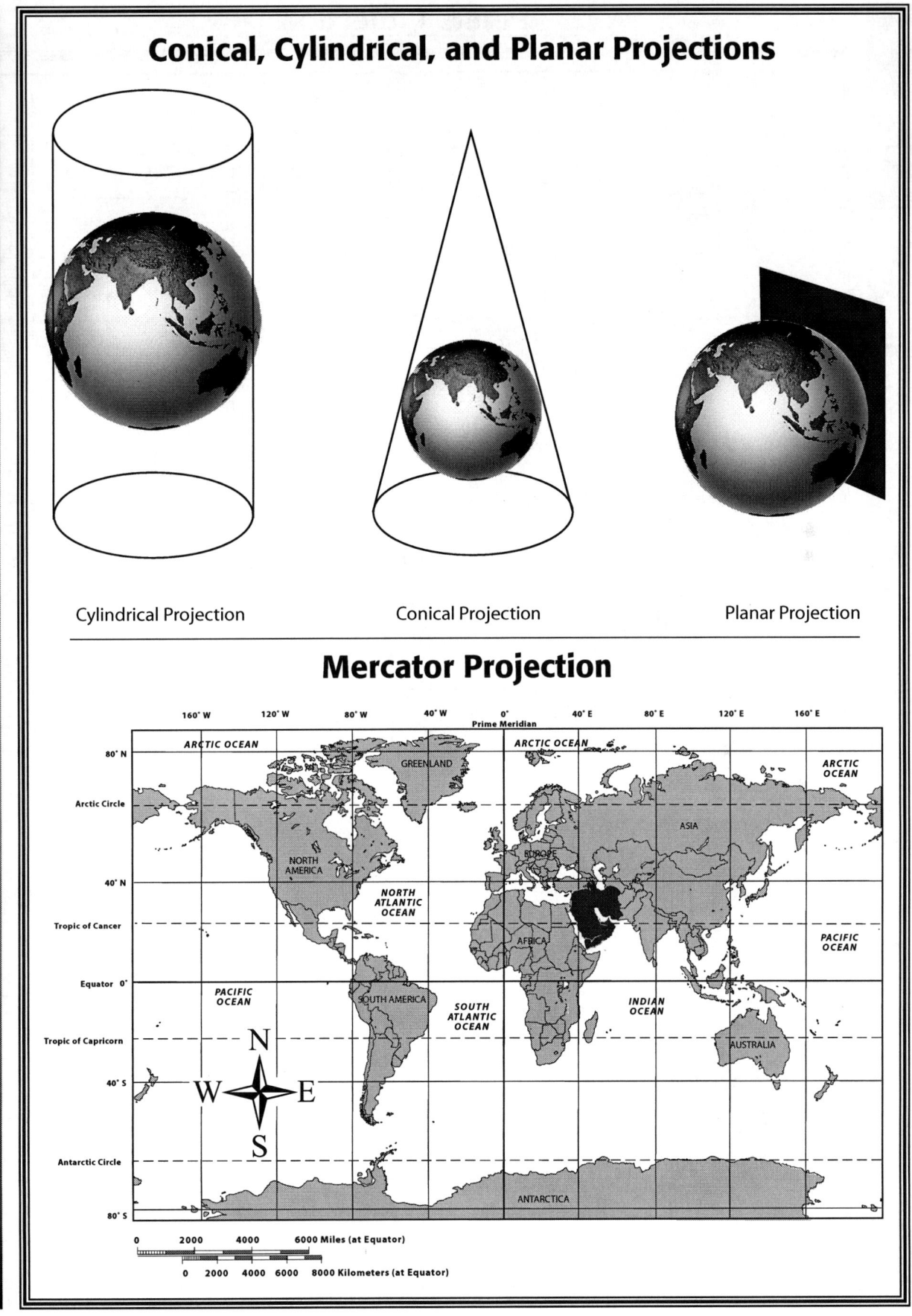

Name: _____

Peters Projection

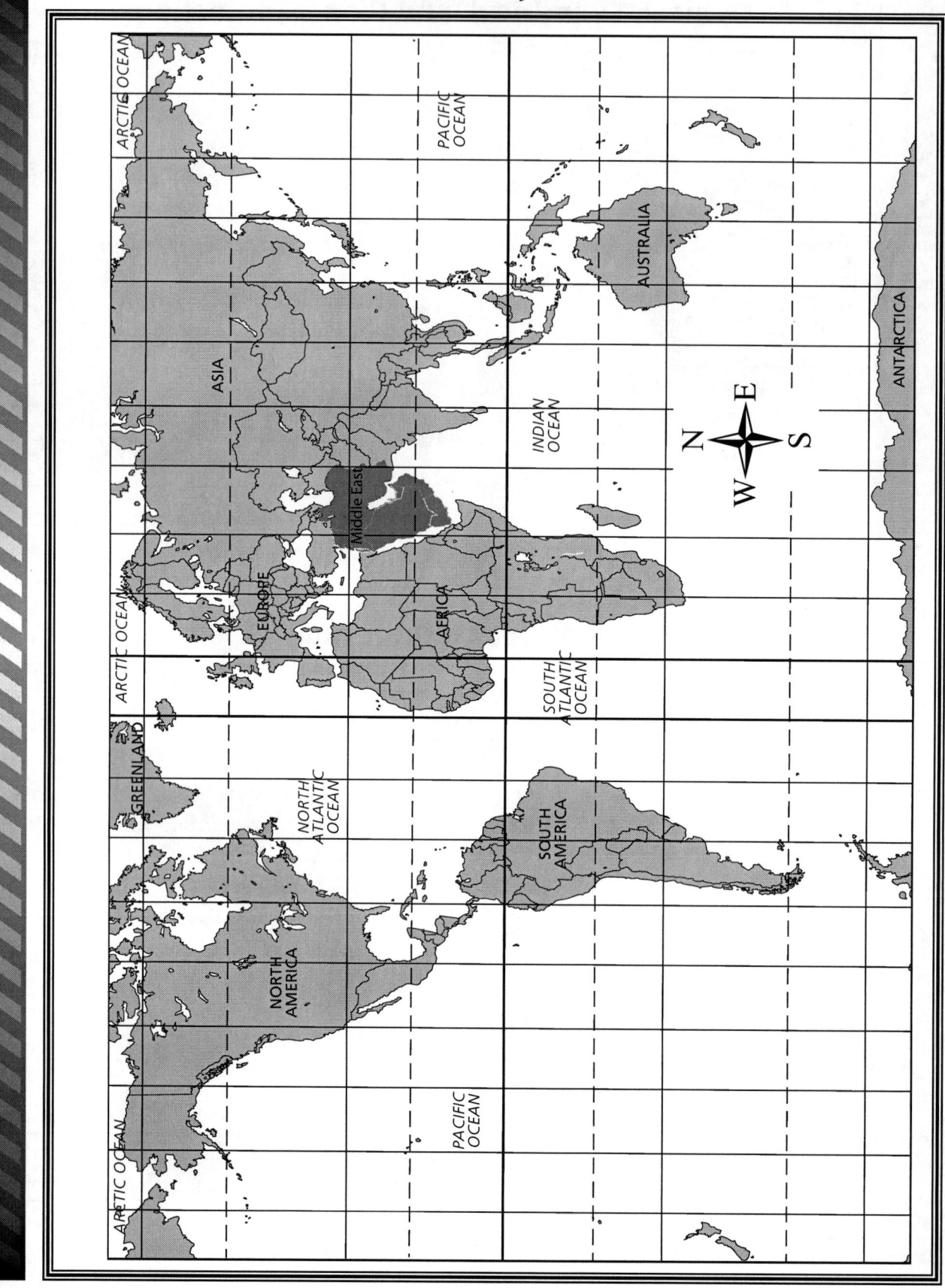

Name: _____

Location of Mecca in Saudi Arabia

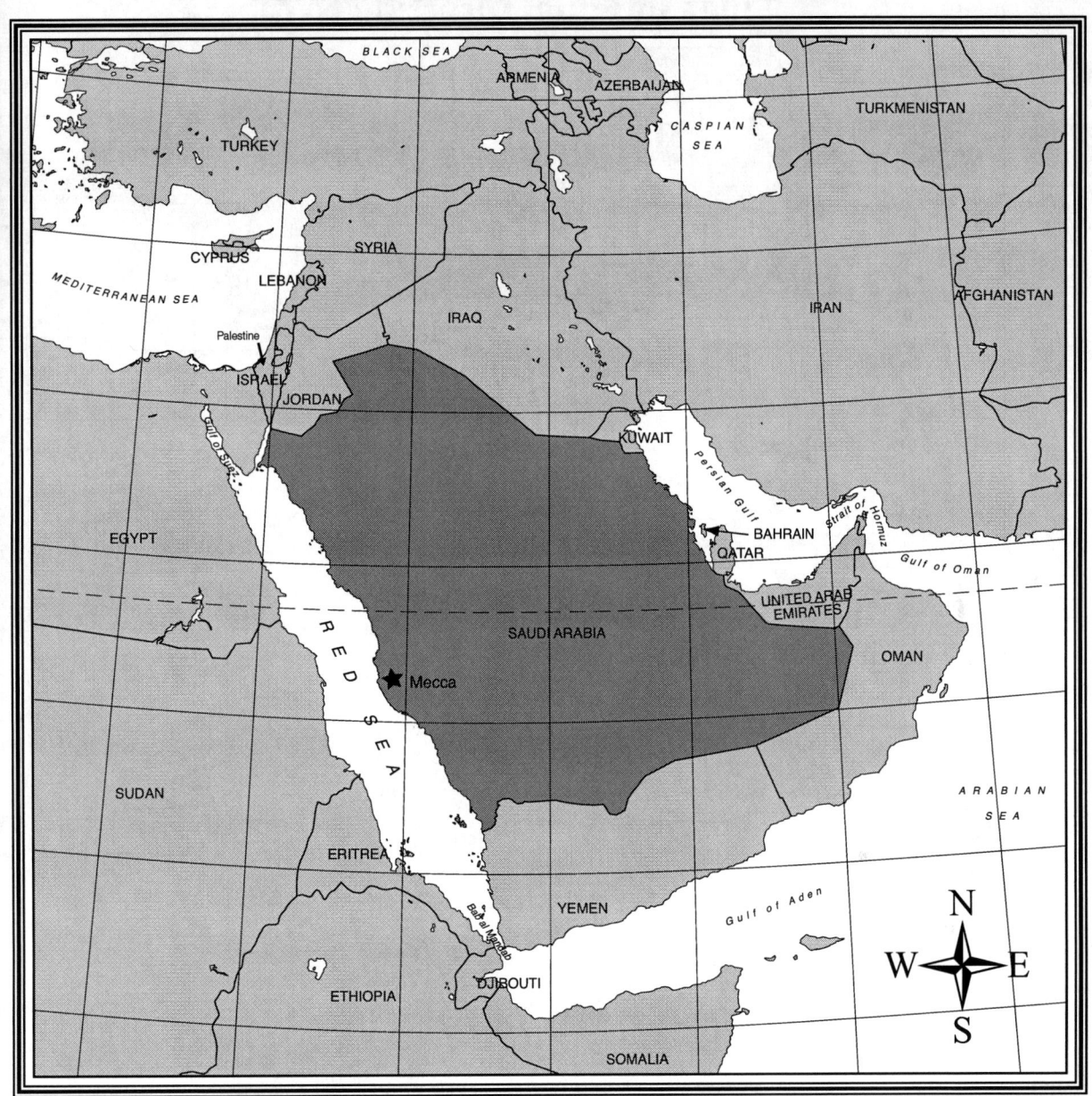

Name: _____

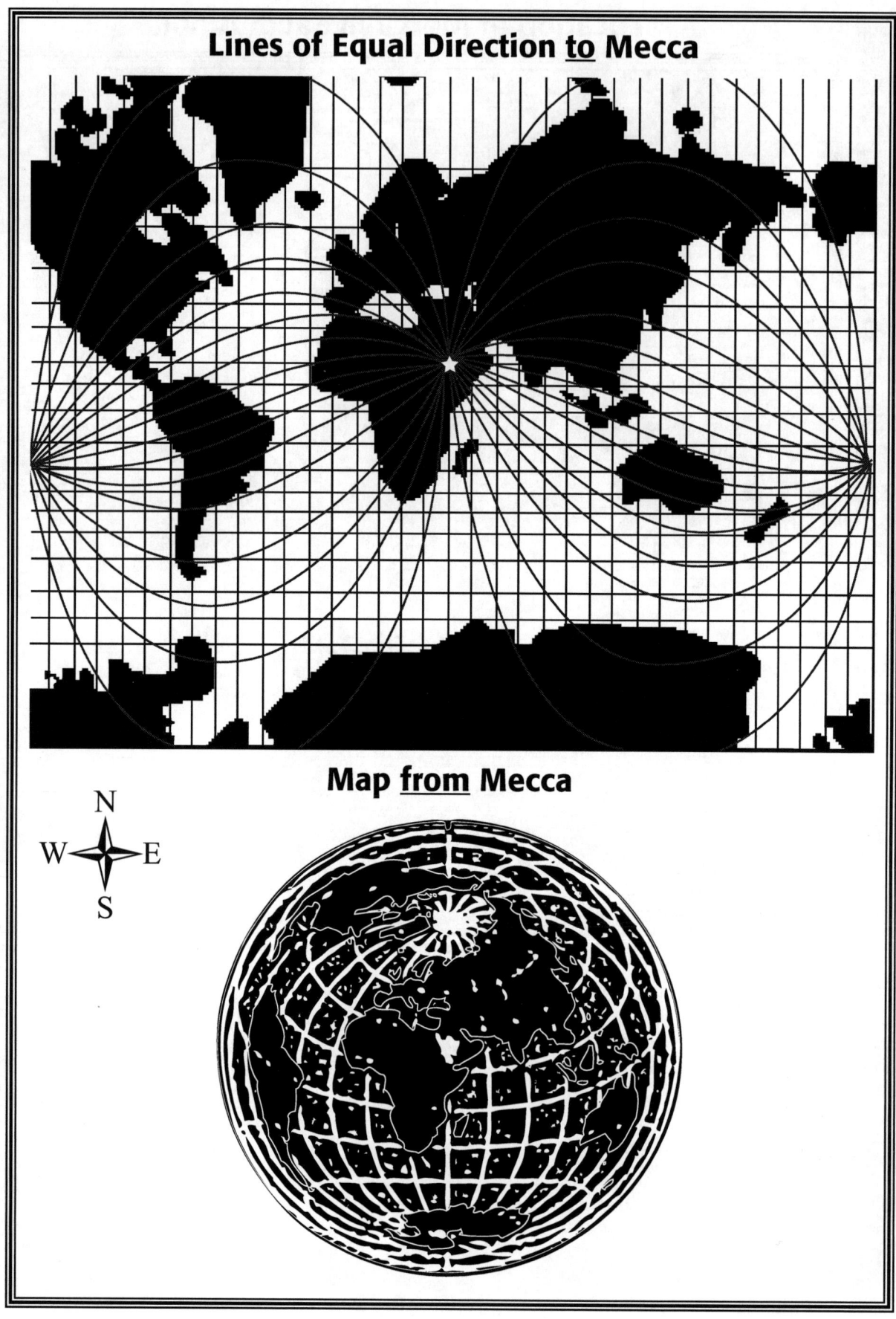

 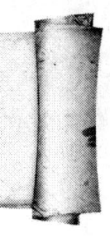

LESSON 5
Mountains and Valleys: Reading a Physical Map

 Goal: To develop concepts and skills related to getting information from a physical map

National Geography Standards

Standard 1. How to use maps and other geographic representations, tools, and technologies to acquire, process, and report information from a spatial perspective.

Preparing Students for Instruction

Before starting this activity, review landforms such as valleys, plains, basins, plateaus, and mountains with students.

Map Overview

This physical map of the Middle East shows landforms as well as rivers and other bodies of water. Ask students to imagine living in each of these areas—the mountains, the deserts, the seacoasts. How would life be different in each area?

Answer Key	
1.	The Tigris and the Euphrates
2.	The Persian Gulf and the Gulf of Oman
3.	Iran
4.	Saudi Arabian land is of varying altitudes. A large portion is from 1,650 to 3,200, but the country also has landforms that are 0 to 1,650 feet above sea level and over 3,200 feet.
5.	The higher elevations, above 6,500 feet, because they are scattered across a large area like a mountain chain, and land that high is usually mountainous
6.	No rivers run through them, and the land is flat.

© 2010 Walch Education   *Critical Thinking About Geography: The Middle East*   **21**

Discussion Guide

To support students in reflecting on the activities and to gather some formative information about student learning, use the following prompts to facilitate a class discussion to "debrief" the map activities.

Prompts/Questions

1. How do you think the landforms of the Middle East affect the life of people who live there?
2. Which altitude do you think would provide the most comfortable lifestyle?

Suggested Appropriate Responses

1. In desert areas, people must wear cool clothing. The clothing should also protect against sunburn. In areas without rivers, people must depend on rainfall as an uncertain water source. They may dig canals to bring water from rivers not too far away, but doing that would probably require international cooperation.
2. Answers may vary. Students may suggest that moderate altitudes would probably have the best climate, and the best water supply.

Extending and Enhancing Learning

- Have students work in groups to make individual physical maps of each country in the Middle East. Have each group prepare a report that shows how the landforms of this country have affected the culture, lifestyle, and economy of the country.

- For students who need more support, have them use the legend and write the altitudes of each marked area on their maps, so they can see where the highlands and lowlands are in the Middle East.

- To challenge students further, have them compare two cities that have similar landforms, for example, Baghdad and Kuwait, both of which are not very much above sea level. Do these cities have water or agricultural problems? What are the major industries, and are they related in any way to the altitude (or lack of altitude) of the land where the cities are located? Is being on a coastline an advantage for Kuwait that Baghdad doesn't have? Other possible pairs are Riyadh and Amman (1,650 to 3,200 feet above sea level) and Damascus and Sanaa (above 6,500 feet). If desired, cities with differing altitudes could also be compared, for example, Tehran and Abu Dhabi, to discover if any of their differences in lifestyle, industry, or agriculture are due to difference in altitude.

Name: _____

 **LESSON 5** — **Mountains and Valleys: Reading a Physical Map**

Geography Vocabulary

basin: a large, bowl-shaped depression in the surface of the land or the ocean floor

gulf: a large area of a sea or ocean partially enclosed by land

physical map: a map that indicates the location of landforms, such as deserts, mountains, plains, and rivers

Reading the Map

This physical map of the Middle East shows land elevations, rivers, and seacoasts of the Middle East. How have the mountains, seacoasts, and rivers affected the way people live in this area?

Understanding the Map

1. What two major rivers flow through Iraq?
2. Land at or just higher than sea level is mostly beside what two bodies of water?
3. The highest landforms in this part of the world are mainly in what country?
4. What altitudes are found in Saudi Arabia?

Analyzing the Map

5. Which altitudes probably indicate mountains? Explain your answer.
6. How can you tell that some of the land in Saudi Arabia, Jordan, Yemen, and Oman is probably desert?

© 2010 Walch Education — Critical Thinking About Geography: The Middle East

Name: _____

Physical Map of the Middle East

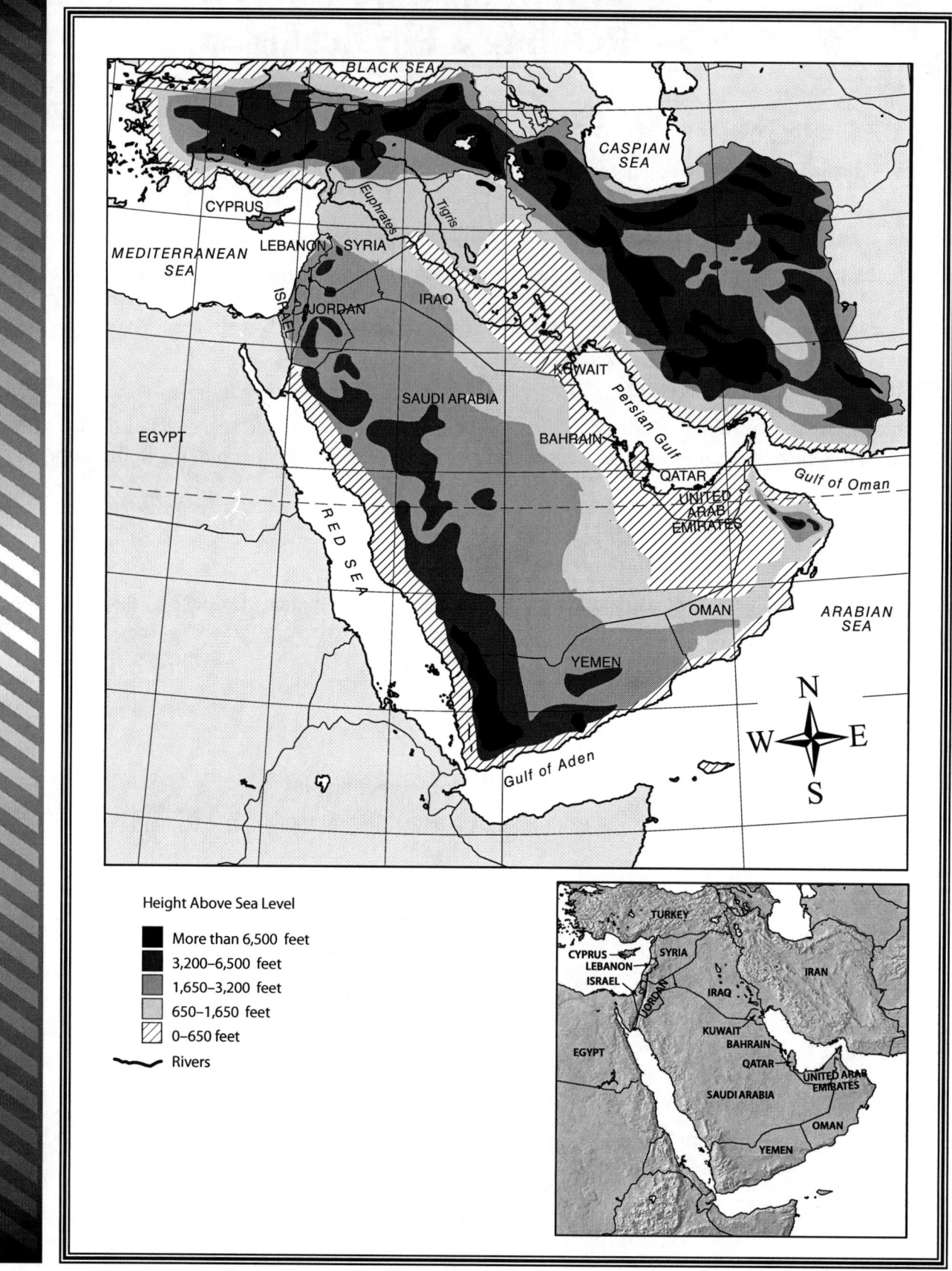

LESSON 6

Exploring Economic Resources and Products

 Goal: To develop concepts and skills related to understanding an economic resources map

National Geography Standards

Standard 1. How to use maps and other geographic representations, tools, and technologies to acquire, process, and report information from a spatial perspective.

Standard 11. The patterns and networks of economic interdependence on Earth's surface.

Standard 16. The changes that occur in the meaning, use, distribution, and importance of resources.

Preparing Students for Instruction

Before starting this activity, review with students how to use the symbols on a map legend to get information from the map.

Map Overview

These two maps show the economic resources and major industries of two countries in the Middle East, Bahrain and Iraq. Bahrain has one large petroleum deposit in the middle of the country. Most of its industry is related to petroleum. Iraq's petroleum deposits are scattered throughout the country. Iraq also has deposits of natural gas. Iraq has pipelines for both petroleum and natural gas, and Bahrain has one petroleum pipeline. These maps demonstrate the importance of petroleum as a resource and an export in the Middle East.

Students should take note that the two maps are in very different scales and that Bahrain is enlarged significantly.

Answer Key
1. Bahrain has only one mineral deposit, a large petroleum field. Iraq has petroleum, natural gas, coal, phosphate, and sulfur.
2. Mosul, Al Qa'im, As Sulaymaniyah, As Samawah, Baghdad, Sinjar, and Karkuk
3. Light industry, food processing, and textiles
4. Baghdad
5. Iraq, because it has more mineral deposits and more industry
6. Food processing industry
7. Bahrain is located near a sea or other large body of navigable water.

© 2010 Walch Education   Critical Thinking About Geography: The Middle East   **25**

Discussion Guide

To support students in reflecting on the activities and to gather some formative information about student learning, use the following prompts to facilitate a class discussion to "debrief" the map activities.

Prompts/Questions

1. What major mineral deposit do these countries share?
2. How do you think having a lot of mineral resources rather than just one helps a country prosper?

Suggested Appropriate Responses

1. Petroleum
2. More resources make more industries possible. The sale of different kinds of products brings in money to the country. If a single resource runs out, then there are others the country can depend on.

Extending and Enhancing Learning

- Have students work in groups to create a map of an imaginary country. The group decides what natural resources this country has, and what industries that are based on those natural resources. Each group then follows these steps: Draw a map and locate cities and a capital city. Make a map legend similar to those on the maps of Iraq and Bahrain, with symbols for resources and symbols for industries. Write three questions about your country that involve resources or industries. Write the answers on a separate sheet of paper. Exchange maps and questions with another group. When the group has decided on the answers to their questions, they may get the "answer key" from the other group.

- For students who need more support, have them write down the cities in each country where each map symbol is located. For example, under the heading "Heavy Industry," they would list each city where that symbol is found on the map. Have students work in pairs or small groups and race the other groups to see which can finish first with the most correct answers.

- To challenge students further, have them research the petroleum industry, including present-day concerns about using up the world's supply. Have teams debate whether running out of petroleum is a real concern. One side supports the idea that if we are careful, we can continue to use petroleum as an energy source, and includes in their argument the economic effects of stopping the use of petroleum. The other side presents information about known petroleum reserves vs. rate of consumption, and supports the use of alternative energy sources.

Name: _____

 **LESSON 6** Exploring Economic Resources and Products

> **Geography Vocabulary**
>
> **industry:** the production and sale of goods
>
> **natural resources:** material occurring in nature, such as coal, oil, and minerals, that can be used to create wealth
>
> **petroleum:** a flammable liquid occurring naturally in deposits under the earth's surface, used to manufacture gasoline and other products

Reading the Maps

These maps of Iraq and Bahrain each give two kinds of information. "Mineral Deposit(s)" shows what natural resources such as petroleum are found in each country. "Industry" shows how each country uses those natural resources and other resources to manufacture goods.

Understanding the Maps

1. What is the main difference between the mineral deposits of Iraq and the mineral deposits of Bahrain?

2. Name the cities where cement is manufactured in Iraq.

3. What three industries are located in the capital city of Bahrain?

4. Which city in Iraq has the most different kinds of industry?

Analyzing the Maps

5. Based on natural resources and industry, which of these two countries is probably wealthier? Explain your thinking.

6. Which industry in Iraq indicates that a large amount of crops may be grown there?

7. What does the fact that shipbuilding and repair are industries in Bahrain tell you about the probable location of that country?

© 2010 Walch Education Critical Thinking About Geography: The Middle East **27**

Name: _____

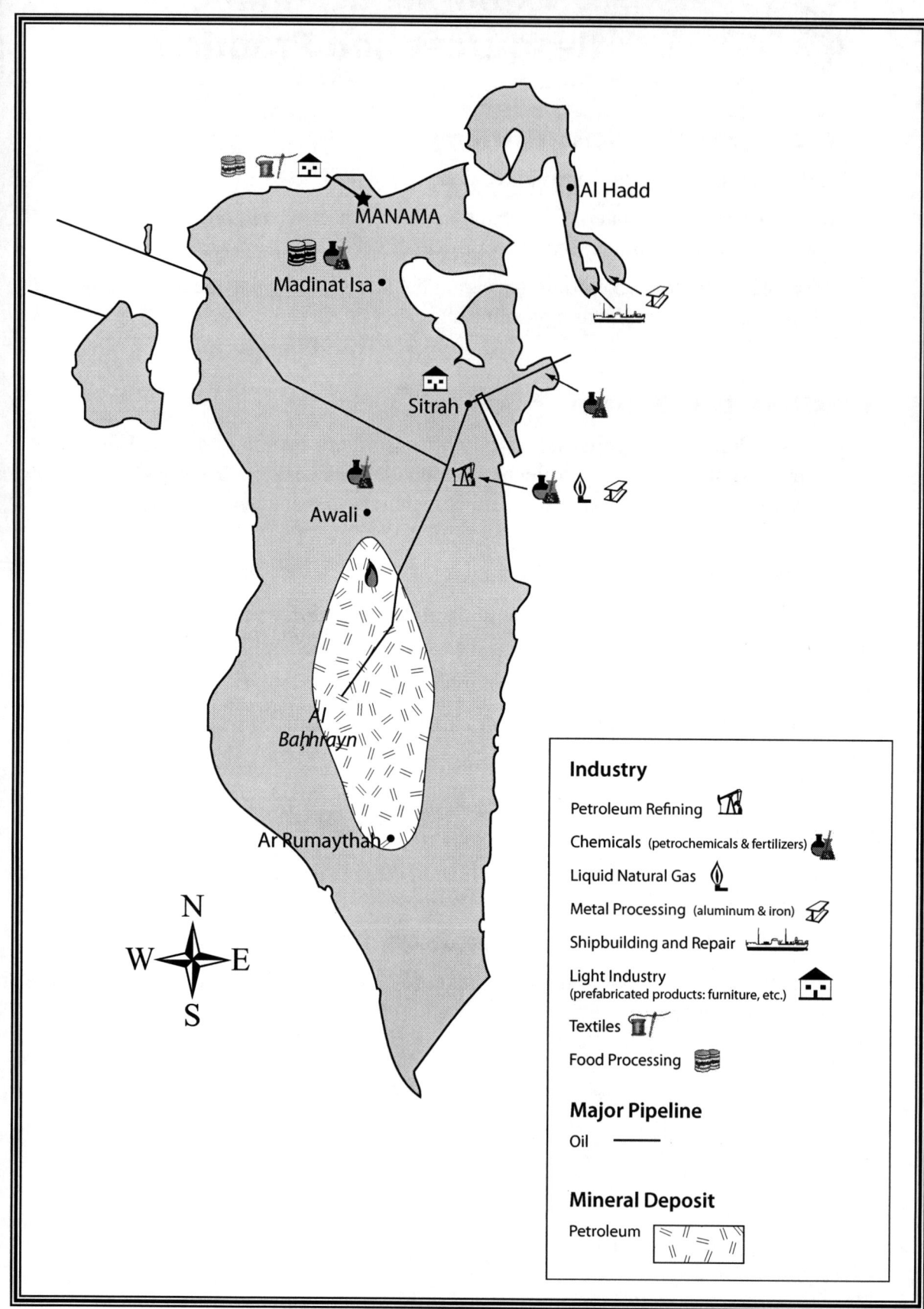

Name: _____

Economic Resources of Iraq

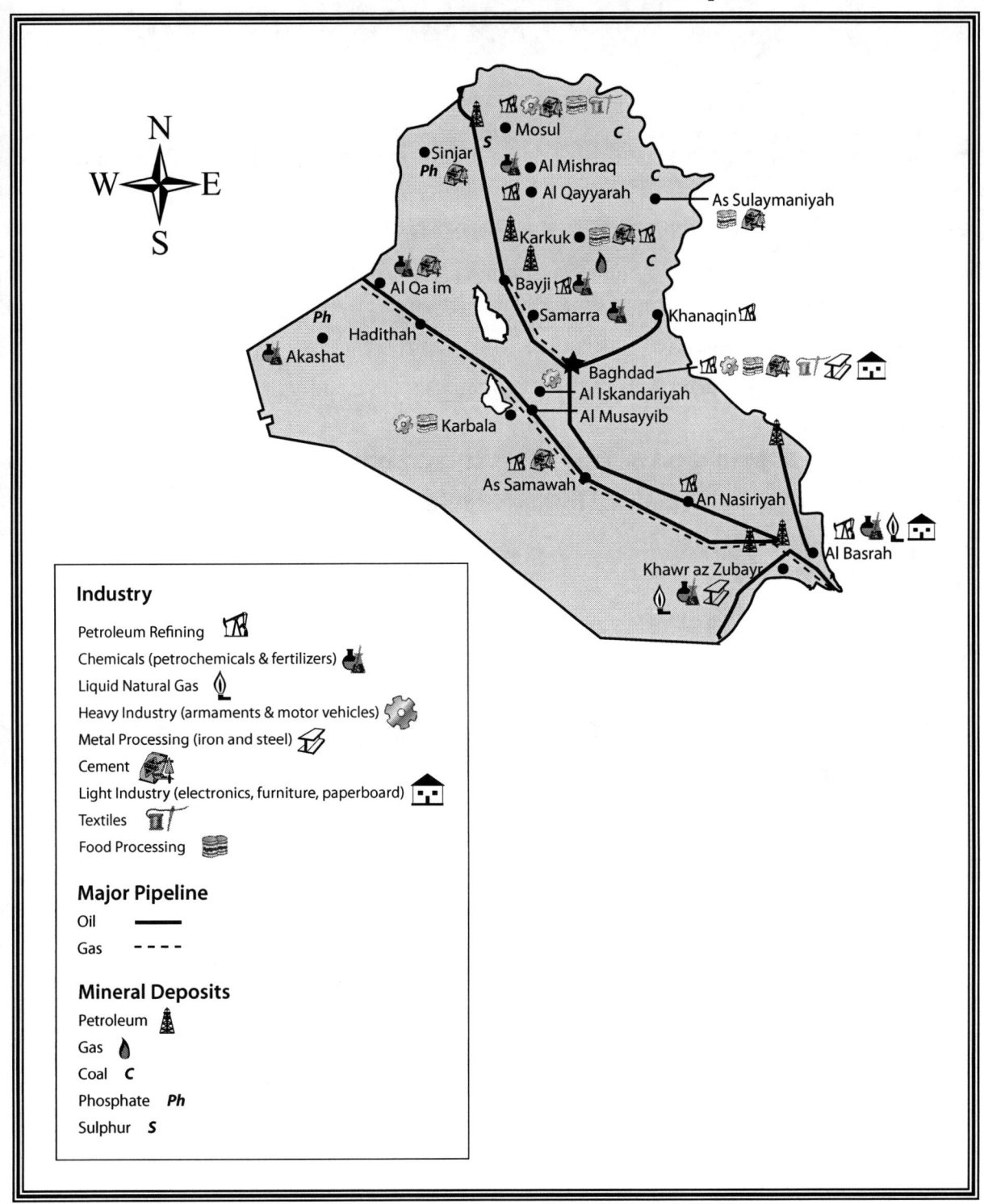

Industry
- Petroleum Refining
- Chemicals (petrochemicals & fertilizers)
- Liquid Natural Gas
- Heavy Industry (armaments & motor vehicles)
- Metal Processing (iron and steel)
- Cement
- Light Industry (electronics, furniture, paperboard)
- Textiles
- Food Processing

Major Pipeline
- Oil
- Gas

Mineral Deposits
- Petroleum
- Gas
- Coal C
- Phosphate Ph
- Sulphur S

LESSON 7

Reading a Land Usage Map

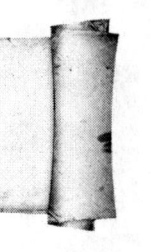

Goal: To develop concepts and skills related to how a group of people use the land where they live

National Geography Standards

Standard 1. How to use maps and other geographic representations, tools, and technologies to acquire, process, and report information from a spatial perspective.

Standard 15. How physical systems affect human systems.

Standard 16. The changes that occur in the meaning, use, distribution, and importance of resources.

Preparing Students for Instruction

Before starting this activity, review map legends with students.

Map Overview

Students will examine how people use landforms and how the landforms influence the foods and other crops produced there.

Answer Key
1. Rough grazing and nomadic herding
2. Rough grazing and nomadic herding
3. The area marked "arable land"
4. Vegetables, fruit, grapes, qat, coffee, cereal, and cotton
5. The water from the oasis makes irrigated farming possible.
6. Answers will vary, but students may infer that the type of land and the probable lack of water make the land unsuitable for growing anything else.

Discussion Guide

To support students in reflecting on the activities and to gather some formative information about student learning, use the following prompts to facilitate a class discussion to "debrief" the map activities.

Prompts/Questions

1. Neither Yemen nor Saudi Arabia has any permanent rivers; instead, they have some dry river beds that fill with water at certain times. Both countries have several oases. How does the distribution of oases affect land usage in these two countries?
2. How do you think people live on the land areas called "Rough grazing/Nomadic herding"?

Suggested Appropriate Responses

1. The scarcity of water in both countries limits the areas where crops can be grown and also limits the types of crops to those that do not require large amounts of water. Both maps show crops clustered around oases.
2. They probably have herds of animals that eat the grass in one area and then move to another area to eat more grass. People live by selling or trading their animals for what they need. They probably live in tents.

Extending and Enhancing Learning

- Have students research land use in other Middle Eastern countries to determine which countries probably generate the most wealth from their land. Have them include information about natural resources and their products in each country. Tell students that a country can gain wealth from land usage and agriculture, but it can also gain wealth from its natural resources. For example, Saudi Arabia is probably the wealthiest Middle Eastern country because of its large supply of petroleum.
- For students who need more support, have them pair up and quiz each other about the two maps. For example, one might ask, "Which country has a large area of arable land?" The partner answers, and then challenges the other with a new question.
- To challenge students further, have them work in groups to research the culture and traditions of the nomadic peoples of the Middle East. They can write their report in the form of a play that demonstrates how these people live and some of the problems they face.

Name: _____

LESSON 7
Reading a Land Usage Map

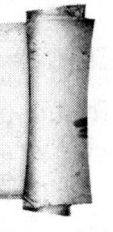

> **Geography Vocabulary**
>
> **arable:** fit for growing crops
>
> **irrigated farming:** bringing water to otherwise dry land in order to plant crops there
>
> **Nomadic:** referring to a group of people who move from place to place with flocks of animals seeking grass for grazing
>
> **oasis:** a place with a water source in an otherwise dry area

✦ Reading the Maps

In a previous lesson, we looked at the landforms of some countries in the Middle East. In this lesson, we are going to examine how people use the landforms of their countries, and whether they modify these landforms to meet their needs. When you look at these maps, first examine the types of land in each country, and then see how people use that land.

✦ Understanding the Maps

1. Besides the wasteland, which is not used, what is the largest area of land usage in Yemen?
2. What is the most common type of land in Saudi Arabia?
3. If you were going to plant a crop in Yemen, where would be the best place to do it?
4. What crops are grown on Yemen's arable land?

✦ Analyzing the Maps

5. Find the oases on the map of Saudi Arabia. Why do you think there is a dark gray area around each oasis? Explain.
6. Why do you think Saudi Arabia produces only four crops? Explain.

Name: _____

Land Usage Map of Yemen

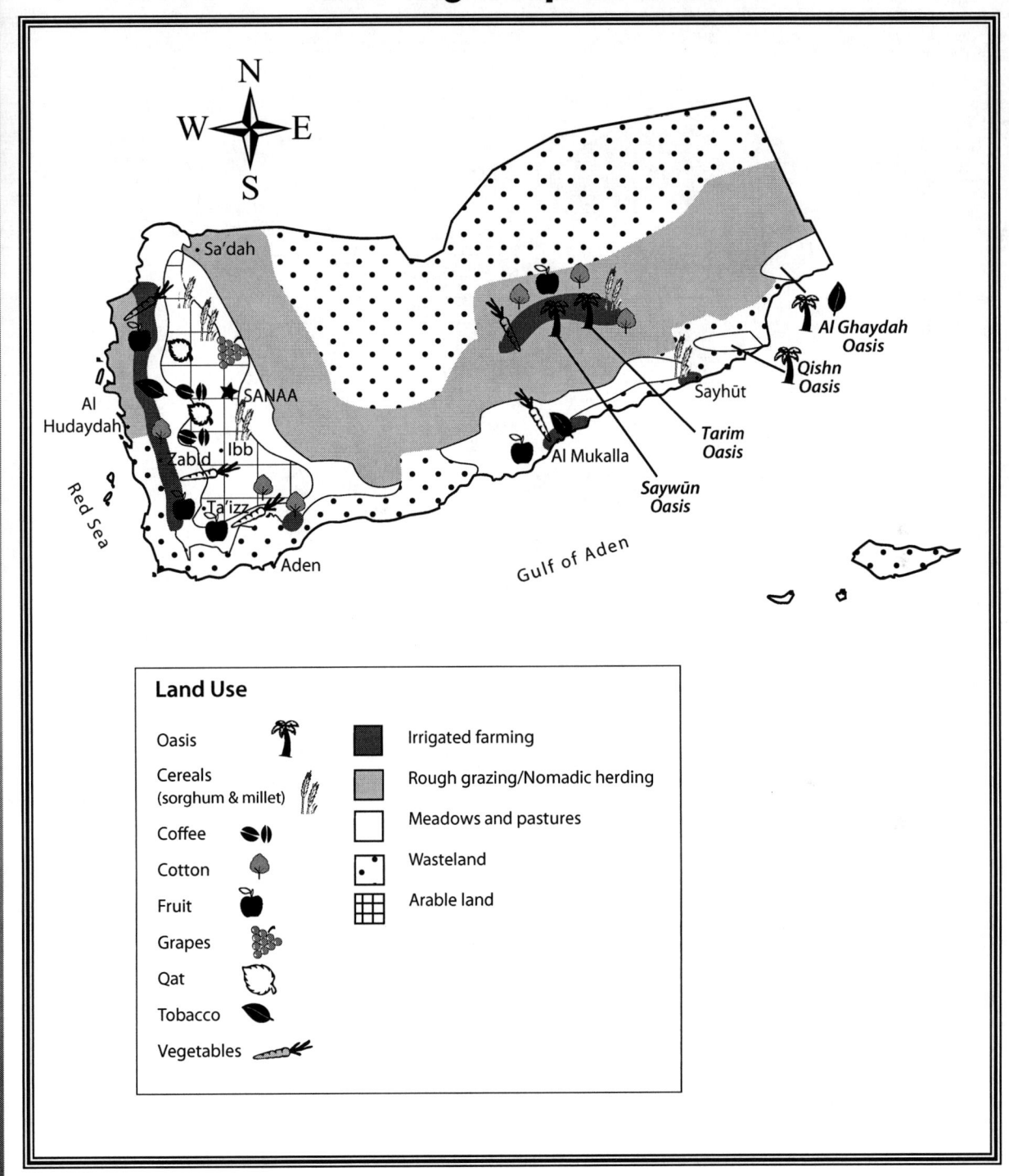

Land Use

- Oasis 🌴
- Cereals (sorghum & millet)
- Coffee
- Cotton
- Fruit 🍎
- Grapes 🍇
- Qat
- Tobacco
- Vegetables 🥕

- Irrigated farming
- Rough grazing/Nomadic herding
- Meadows and pastures
- Wasteland
- Arable land

© 2010 Walch Education — Critical Thinking About Geography: The Middle East

Name: _____

Land Usage Map of Saudi Arabia

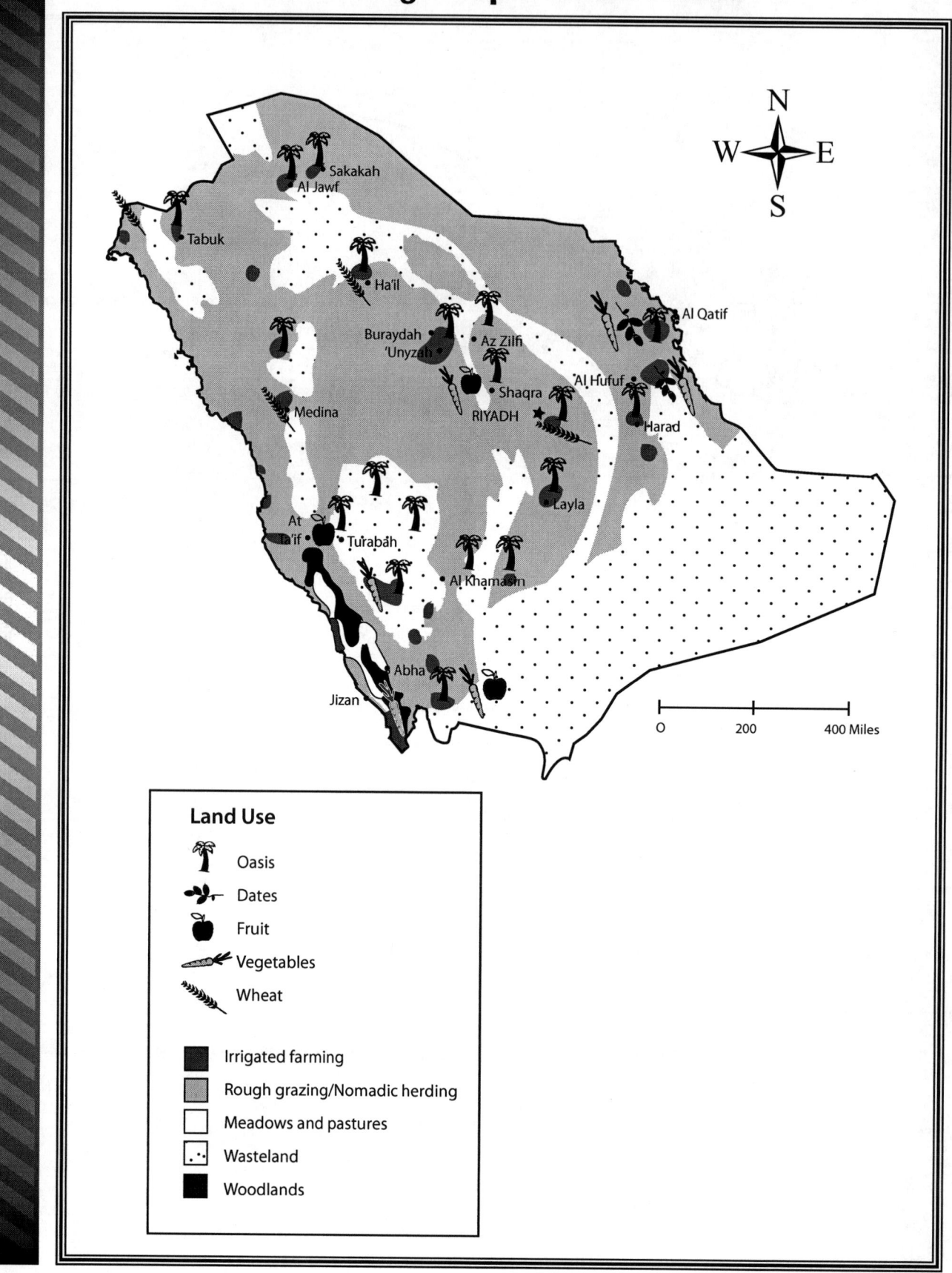

Land Use
- Oasis
- Dates
- Fruit
- Vegetables
- Wheat
- Irrigated farming
- Rough grazing/Nomadic herding
- Meadows and pastures
- Wasteland
- Woodlands

34   *Critical Thinking About Geography: The Middle East*   © 2010 Walch Education

LESSON 8

Reading a Highway Map

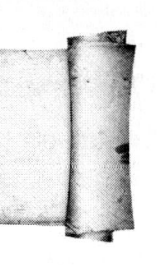

Goal: To develop concepts and skills related to locating places on a map, planning a route, understanding symbols in a legend, and using map scale to measure distance

National Geography Standards

Standard 1. How to use maps and other geographic representations, tools, and technologies to acquire, process, and report information from a spatial perspective.

Standard 3. How to analyze the spatial organization of people, places, and environments on Earth's surface.

Preparing Students for Instruction

Before starting this activity, review with students how to measure distance on a map using a ruler and the map scale.

Map Overview

This map shows the country of Lebanon and parts of neighboring Syria, and the network of roads and railroads that join cities.

Answer Key
1. The expressway begins in Tripoli and extends along the coast to Ez Zahrani, where it turns inland.
2. About 30 miles
3. Halba
4. In 1948, Israel and Lebanon fought each other in the Arab-Israeli War. A 1949 armistice established boundary lines for each country, but it was not an official border.
5. You would take the expressway from Tripoli to Antilyas, then the road from Antilyas to Zahle. Finally, you would need to take a train from Zahle to Rayak.
6. Beirut
7. Answers will vary. Damascus has a good source of water that may have caused people to settle there. Beirut is on the coast, located in a position to control shipping as well as to keep away enemies who might come by sea.

© 2010 Walch Education   Critical Thinking About Geography: The Middle East   **35**

Discussion Guide

To support students in reflecting on the activities and to gather some formative information about student learning, use the following prompts to facilitate a class discussion to "debrief" the map activities.

Prompts/Questions

1. When do we use highway maps?
2. Do you think a driving trip in Lebanon would be easy or challenging? Why?

Suggested Appropriate Responses

1. We use them when traveling somewhere new or unfamiliar. We use them to plan a trip or to guide us on the road.
2. Answers will vary. Some students may say it would be easy because there is a long expressway along the coast. Some will say it would be challenging because it is clear on the map that most of the roads have many curves, and there is only one expressway in the whole country.

Extending and Enhancing Learning

- Have students study road maps of other Middle Eastern countries, such as the road maps of Israel, Cyprus, Oman, and Qatar that accompany this lesson. Divide students into an even number of teams. Each team receives a map of one country and works to ask five or six questions about that map, similar to the questions in this lesson. The team records the answers separately, and then exchanges map and questions with another team. Team A will correct Team B's answers and the reverse. Teams with the most correct answers will be declared winners. Caution students against asking obscure or overly difficult questions.

- For students who need more support, have them plan short trips from one city in Lebanon to two others, naming the cities and measuring distances using the map scale.

- To challenge students further, have them plan a road trip throughout Lebanon, from one end to the other, listing the cities they will pass through and where they will stop for the night after 100 miles or so. If desired, they could include a side trip to Syria. Students can write a journal of this imaginary trip, using information gathered about places in Lebanon from the Internet.

Name: _____

LESSON 8
Reading a Highway Map

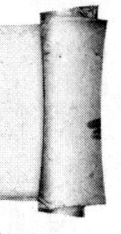

> **Geography Vocabulary**
> **expressway:** a major divided highway with few intersections

✦ Reading the Map

This map of Lebanon and part of Syria shows the network of roads, expressways, and railroads that connect places in these countries. The map scale allows us to measure distance on the map and convert those measurements to real distance on land.

✦ Understanding the Map

1. The map shows only one expressway in Lebanon. Name the northern city where this expressway begins. What is the last coastal city before the expressway turns inland?

2. Use the legend and a ruler to find the approximate distance in miles between Beirut and Ez Zahrani. Your answer will not be precise because there are some curves in the road.

3. Find a city that is just about 15 miles northeast of Tripoli.

✦ Analyzing the Map

4. An armistice is an agreement to stop fighting. It means that neither side wins; they just don't fight any more. What does the southern boundary of Lebanon tell you about its past relations with Israel? Explain your thinking.

5. Plan a driving trip from Tripoli to Rayak. Use the expressway for the longest leg of your trip, then switch to a regular road. Once you arrive in Zahle, how would you travel from there to Rayak?

6. Two sets of railroad tracks leave the city of Hims in Syria. One goes west to the coast and then south along the coast of Lebanon. The other goes inland in a southwest direction. Eventually they come together. Trace each route. Near what major city do they meet?

7. Capital cities usually arise for reasons that are important to the people who settle there. What would attract settlers to each of the capital cities shown on this map? Explain.

© 2010 Walch Education   Critical Thinking About Geography: The Middle East   **37**

Name: _____

Highway Map of Lebanon

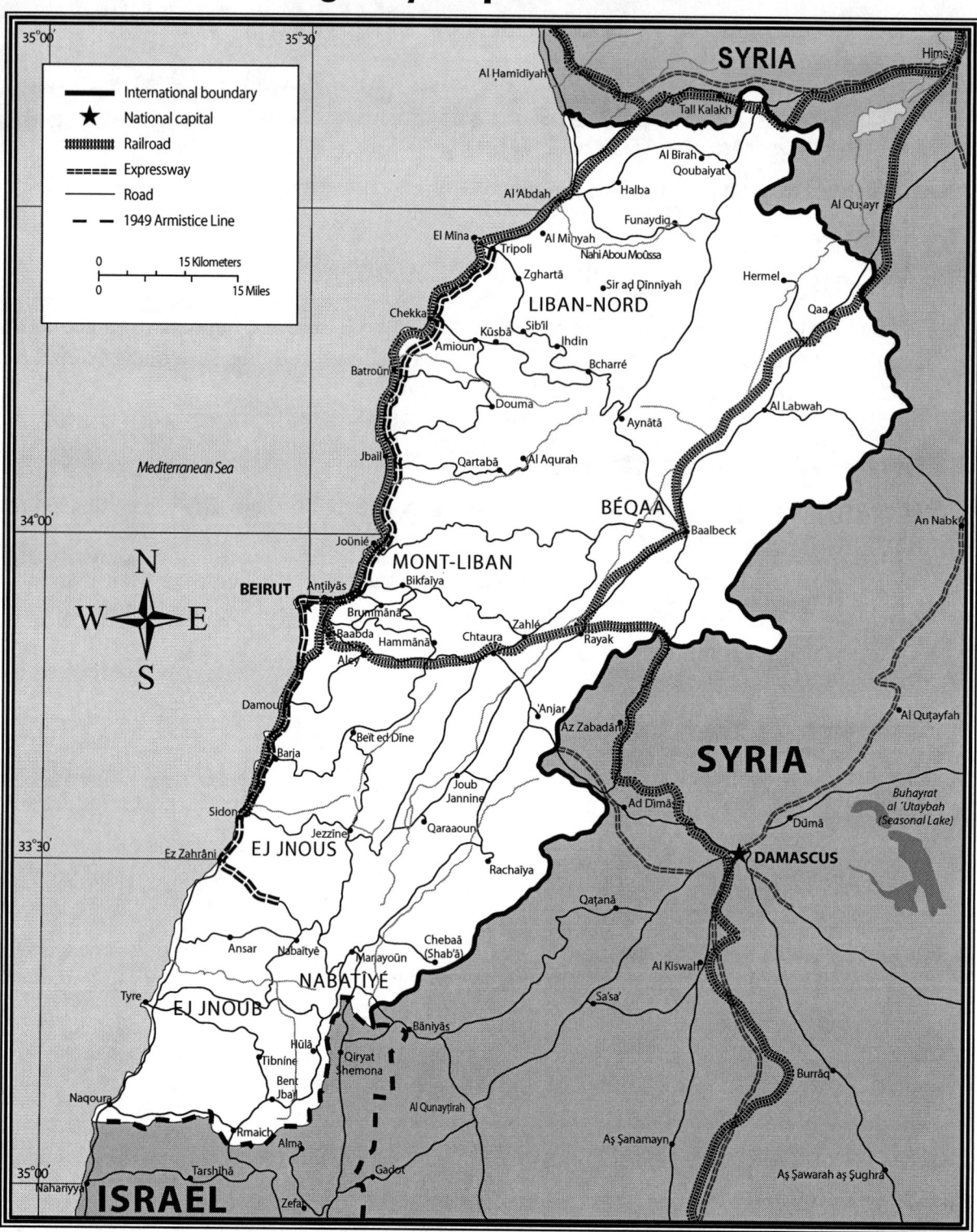

LESSON 9: Understanding Population Density

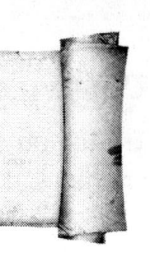

Goal: To develop concepts and skills related to deriving information from a population density map

National Geography Standards

Standard 1. How to use maps and other geographic representations, tools, and technologies to acquire, process, and report information from a spatial perspective.

Standard 3. How to analyze the spatial organization of people, places, and environments on Earth's surface.

Preparing Students for Instruction

Before starting this activity, review the following with students:

- Make sure students know how to use the map legend to find and interpret areas and resources on a map.

Map Overview

This population density map of Yemen is paired with the land usage map so that students can understand the reasons why a large portion of the country seems uninhabited. The nomadic groups that move with their grazing animals are probably not counted in a census of the country's population. The land affects where people choose to live.

Answer Key
1. The wasteland and the nomadic grazing and herding areas
2. Between 260 and 400 persons per square mile
3. Sanaa and Al Hudaydah
4. Population means the total number of people living in an area such as a town or city. Population density means the average number of people in a smaller given area, such as one square kilometer or one square mile.
5. Answers will vary, but students may say that the nomadic lifestyle, where people move frequently so their animals can graze, requires a large area of land for the use of each person/family group and their herd of animals. Also, very few, if any, people would live in the wasteland.
6. Based on the land usage map, probably most people in the eastern part of Yemen are engaged in some kind of agricultural work.

Discussion Guide

To support students in reflecting on the activities and to gather some formative information about student learning, use the following prompts to facilitate a class discussion to "debrief" the map activities.

Prompts/Questions

1. What relationship do you see between land use and population density?
2. Why might it be hard to determine how many people live in the nomadic grazing areas?

Suggested Appropriate Responses

1. Answers will vary. Students may say that areas where the land is productive tend to have greater population density. People live there because they can find work and earn a living there.
2. They do not have houses and would be hard to locate because they move so often.

Extending and Enhancing Learning

- Have students make maps of the population density of the school, or of a wing of the school building. Have them research the square footage of a typical classroom and find out the number of students in each class. If students change classrooms during the day, have them select a period to calculate (e.g., population density of the left wing of the school during seventh period). Have students make a map legend. Which classroom has the greatest population density? Why?

- For students who need more support, have them examine population density maps for other countries in the Middle East. Have them search for reasons why some areas have greater population densities than others.

- To challenge students further, have them research population density statistics for urban, suburban, and rural areas in a country of their choice, and develop explanations for the differences in population density. Have them consider housing as a factor of population density. In a large city with a dense population, people may live in large apartment buildings. In rural areas, people may live almost isolated, in single houses surrounded by a great deal of land.

Name: _____

LESSON 9
Understanding Population Density

Geography Vocabulary

population density: the number of people living in a given amount of space

✦ Reading the Maps

Population density means how many people live in a certain amount of space. Examine this population density map of Yemen. Think about why people have chosen to live in certain areas of the country. Why is a large portion of the country almost uninhabited? Compare the population density map with the land usage map of the same country. Some land is more habitable. Some lifestyles require large areas of land.

✦ Understanding the Maps

1. Which land use areas in Yemen have 0 to 26 people per square mile?
2. What is the population density per square mile of the area surrounding Ta'izz?
3. Name two cities in areas with a population density between 130 and 259 people per square mile.

✦ Analyzing the Maps

4. What is the difference between the population of a city and the population density of an area? Explain.
5. Why do you think the area marked in white on the population density map and in black and dark gray on the land usage map has so few people per square mile?
6. What kind of work do you think supports the relatively large population density in the eastern region of Yemen? Use the land usage map to help you answer this question.

© 2010 Walch Education   Critical Thinking About Geography: The Middle East   41

Name: _____

Population Density Map of Yemen

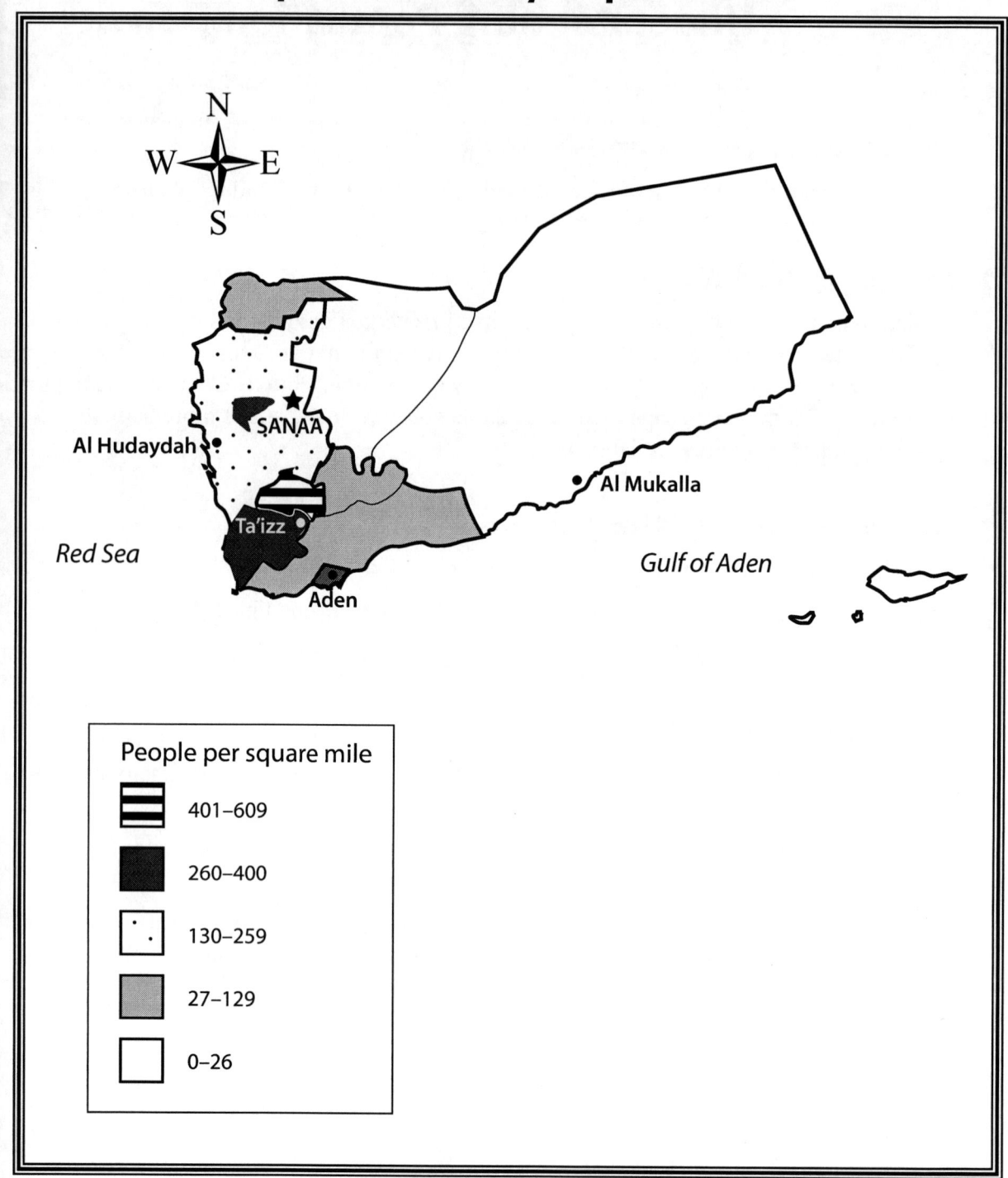

Name: _____

Land Usage Map of Yemen

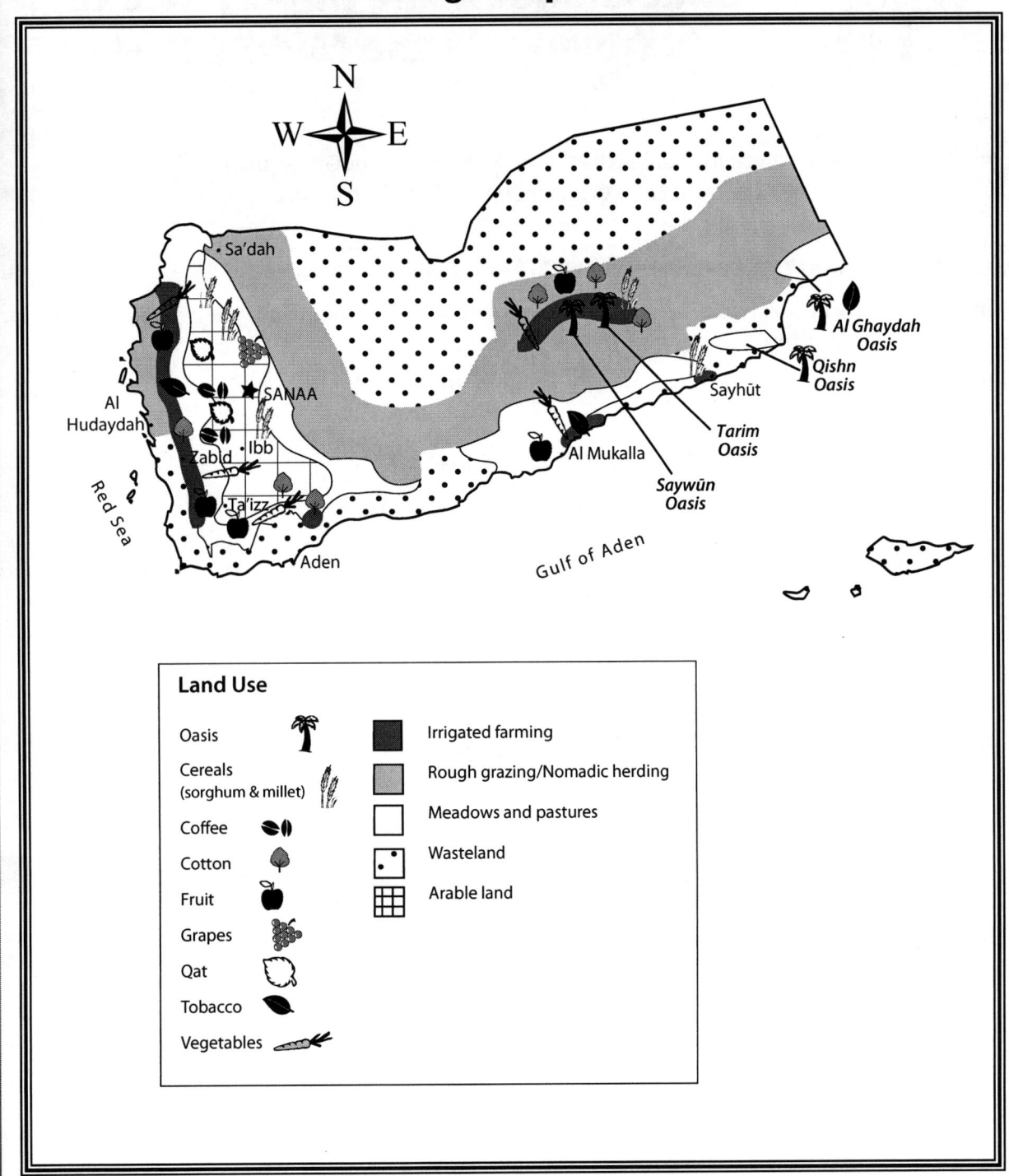

Land Use

Symbol	Type
Oasis	🌴
Cereals (sorghum & millet)	🌾
Coffee	☕
Cotton	
Fruit	🍎
Grapes	🍇
Qat	
Tobacco	
Vegetables	🥕

- Irrigated farming
- Rough grazing/Nomadic herding
- Meadows and pastures
- Wasteland
- Arable land

© 2010 Walch Education — Critical Thinking About Geography: The Middle East

LESSON 10
Understanding the Importance of Petroleum in the Middle East

Goal: To develop concepts and skills related to using a production map to understand the importance of petroleum to the economy of the Middle East

National Geography Standards

Standard 1. How to use maps and other geographic representations, tools, and technologies to acquire, process, and report information from a spatial perspective.

Standard 16. The changes that occur in the meaning, use, distribution, and importance of resources.

Preparing Students for Instruction

Before starting this activity, review with students what they may know about economic resources in Bahrain and Iraq. Petroleum is the major economic resource of Bahrain. Iraq also has a number of petroleum deposits. Countries with large supplies of petroleum may be expected to be the largest producers of petroleum products. (See Lesson 6 for more information on resources in these two countries.)

Map Overview

This map shows production of petroleum and related products in countries of the Middle East in terms of the number of barrels per day.

Answer Key
1. Saudi Arabia
2. Qatar
3. 1,958,000 barrels per day
4. Cyprus, Israel, Lebanon, and Jordan
5. Jordan is landlocked and cannot ship directly by sea. Iraq is nearly landlocked and has limited capacity to ship directly by sea. The other countries have coastlines that give ample opportunity to ship by sea.
6. Most likely these countries have a larger amount of petroleum resources than the other countries.

Discussion Guide

To support students in reflecting on the activities and to gather some formative information about student learning, use the following prompts to facilitate a class discussion to "debrief" the map activities.

Prompts/Questions

1. Petroleum is called a non-renewable resource because there is only a certain amount of it, and there will never be more. What is likely to happen to petroleum-producing countries when their supply of petroleum is exhausted?
2. What may happen to petroleum-producing countries when the countries they usually supply cut back on their need for petroleum by turning to alternative energy sources such as wind or solar power?

Suggested Appropriate Responses

1. Answers will vary. Students may say that these countries will produce alternative fuels, or use other natural resources as main products.
2. Answers will vary, but students should suggest that the economies would suffer if the demand for petroleum decreases. The price of petroleum may also go down if demand decreases.

Extending and Enhancing Learning

+ Have students research other countries in the world that produce petroleum and refine it. How does their production compare with that in the Middle East? Students can research national wealth statistics to discover whether petroleum refining produces more wealth than other kinds of production. For example, how does it compare with diamond mining in South Africa?
+ For students who need more support, have them list the countries on this map in order of production, from least to greatest, and include the number of barrels per day.
+ To challenge students further, have them research the process of refining petroleum and make a graphic indicator that shows the steps and results. Petroleum sales are commonly listed per barrel. How much refined petroleum is in a barrel (quarts, gallons, liters)?

Name: _____

LESSON 10
Understanding the Importance of Petroleum in the Middle East

Geography Vocabulary

barrels per day: the number of barrels of petroleum produced in a single day

✦ Reading the Map

Look at the maps. Petroleum is an important resource of many countries in the Middle East. Petroleum is refined into gasoline and other products. It is exported to countries around the world. It is the main source of wealth for many Middle Eastern countries. This map compares petroleum (and natural gas) production in terms of how many barrels are produced each day in a country's refineries.

✦ Understanding the Map

1. Looking just at the sizes of the barrels, which country refines the most petroleum?
2. Which country produces more petroleum and natural gas, Qatar or Syria?
3. How many barrels per day are produced in Iraq?
4. Which countries on this map do not refine petroleum?

✦ Analyzing the Map

5. What problems might Iraq and Jordan have shipping their refined petroleum that other Middle Eastern countries would not have? Explain.
6. Why do you think some countries refine more petroleum than other countries? Explain.

Name: _____

Middle East Production of Petroleum and Related Products (Natural Gas, Oil)

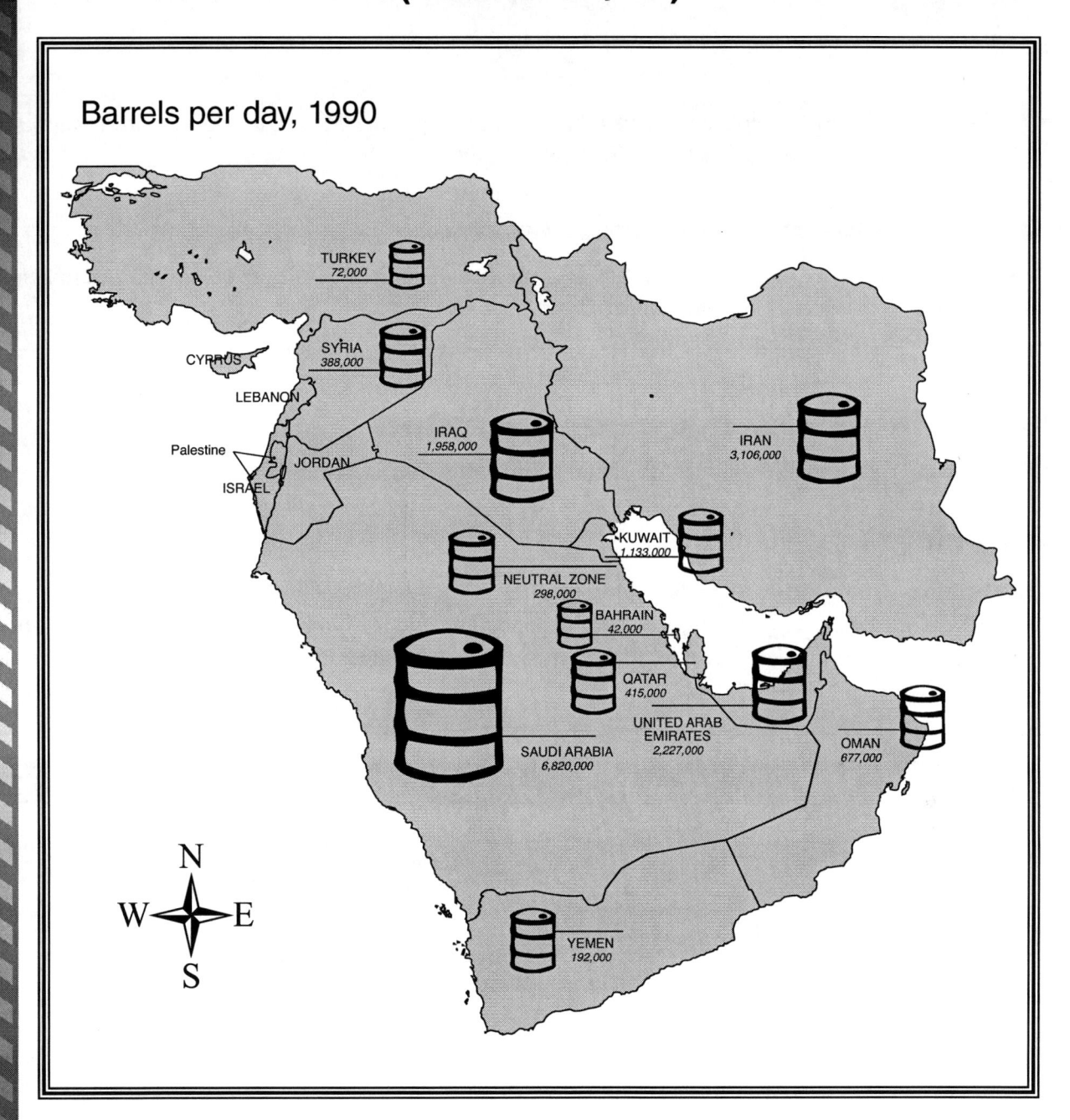

Barrels per day, 1990

- TURKEY 72,000
- SYRIA 388,000
- CYPRUS
- LEBANON
- Palestine
- ISRAEL
- JORDAN
- IRAQ 1,958,000
- IRAN 3,106,000
- KUWAIT 1,133,000
- NEUTRAL ZONE 298,000
- BAHRAIN 42,000
- QATAR 415,000
- SAUDI ARABIA 6,820,000
- UNITED ARAB EMIRATES 2,227,000
- OMAN 677,000
- YEMEN 192,000

© 2010 Walch Education — Critical Thinking About Geography: The Middle East

LESSON 11

Reading a Climate Map

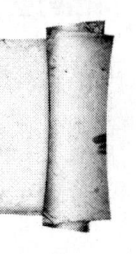

✦ **Goal:** To develop concepts and skills related to reading climate maps and using information on them to compare climates in different seasons

National Geography Standards

Standard 1. How to use maps and other geographic representations, tools, and technologies to acquire, process, and report information from a spatial perspective.

Standard 7. The physical processes that shape the patterns of Earth's surface.

Preparing Students for Instruction

Before starting this activity, review with students how to get information from a chart or table.

Map Overview

These two maps show the average daily temperatures in selected cities in the Middle East. The temperatures are shown in two ways, as shadings on a map and as numbers on a chart. Seasonal changes can be observed and calculated because the maps show January and July temperatures, that is, the warmest and coldest times of the year.

Answer Key
1. 70°F
2. Riyadh's average daily high temperature in January is 70°F. In July, the average is 107°F. 107 − 70 = 37°F
3. Ankara, Turkey, 24°F
4. Baghdad, Iraq, 110°F
5. Near a body of water, temperatures are more consistent with less seasonal change and tend to be cooler in summer.
6. The city nearest the equator is Sanaa, Yemen, with an average high in July of 81°F. The city farthest north of the equator is Istanbul, Turkey, with an average high in July of 81°F. Students should conclude that factors other than closeness to the equator affect the summer average high temperatures in the Middle East.

48 *Critical Thinking About Geography: The Middle East* © 2010 Walch Education

Discussion Guide

To support students in reflecting on the activities and to gather some formative information about student learning, use the following prompts to facilitate a class discussion to "debrief" the map activities.

Prompts/Questions

1. Did you find it easier to read the temperatures using the map shadings or using the charts? Why?
2. As you can tell from the maps and charts, the Middle East is a very hot part of the world. How do you think people keep cool there?

Suggested Appropriate Responses

1. Students may find either one easier. Using the chart gives a more precise number. The map shadings only give a range and are not always precise for a given city.
2. Answers will vary, but may include wearing cool clothing, using fans and air conditioning, and drinking cool drinks. Students may add that people who live there are used to the climate and it may not feel as hot to them as it would to a visitor from a cooler climate.

Extending and Enhancing Learning

- Arrange students in groups. Assign one group to research average maximum and minimum temperatures for colder parts of the world, such as Alaska or the South Pole. Assign several other groups to research temperatures for countries with intermediate climates. When research is complete, have each group share their results. Then have students create a chart similar to the one accompanying the map. The chart should rank the countries' climates in order from coldest to warmest. Display the chart in the classroom.

- For students who need more support, have them locate on the map cities with certain average maximum or minimum temperatures, and countries where those cities are located with certain ranges of temperature. For example, ask, "What is the range of temperatures in January for Saudi Arabia? Do the maximum and minimum temperatures for Riyadh fall within that range?" Students can then arrange cities or countries in order on a chart, from coldest to warmest or the reverse.

- To challenge students further, have them research changing climates for the whole planet over millions of years (e.g., ice ages and warmer ages).

Name: _____

LESSON 11
Reading a Climate Map

> **Geography Vocabulary**
>
> **average daily temperature:** the average of the high and low temperatures for a given day
>
> **average maximum temperature:** the average of the high temperatures for a given period
>
> **average minimum temperature:** the average of low temperatures for a given period
>
> **average monthly temperature:** the average of the "average daily temperatures" for a given month

✦ Reading the Maps

These two maps show the average daily temperatures in some areas of the Middle East. They show the average high temperatures and the average low temperatures for January and July, the coldest and warmest months. You can use the map legend to find the averages for a whole country, or use the chart to find averages for certain cities. The first map shows winter temperatures, and the second map shows summer temperatures.

✦ Understanding the Maps

1. What is the average daily high temperature in Riyadh in January?

2. What is the difference between the average daily high temperature in Riyadh in January and the average daily high temperature in Riyadh in July?

3. Which city in which country has the lowest average minimum temperature in January, and what is that temperature?

4. Which city in which country has the highest average maximum temperature in July, and what is that temperature?

✦ Analyzing the Maps

5. How does being near a body of water—for example, as in Yemen—seem to affect the winter and summer climates?

6. How does location near the equator seem to affect the average temperatures in July? Find the city closest to the equator, and compare it to the city located on an island in the Mediterranean Sea.

50 Critical Thinking About Geography: The Middle East © 2010 Walch Education

Climate Maps of the Middle East in January and July

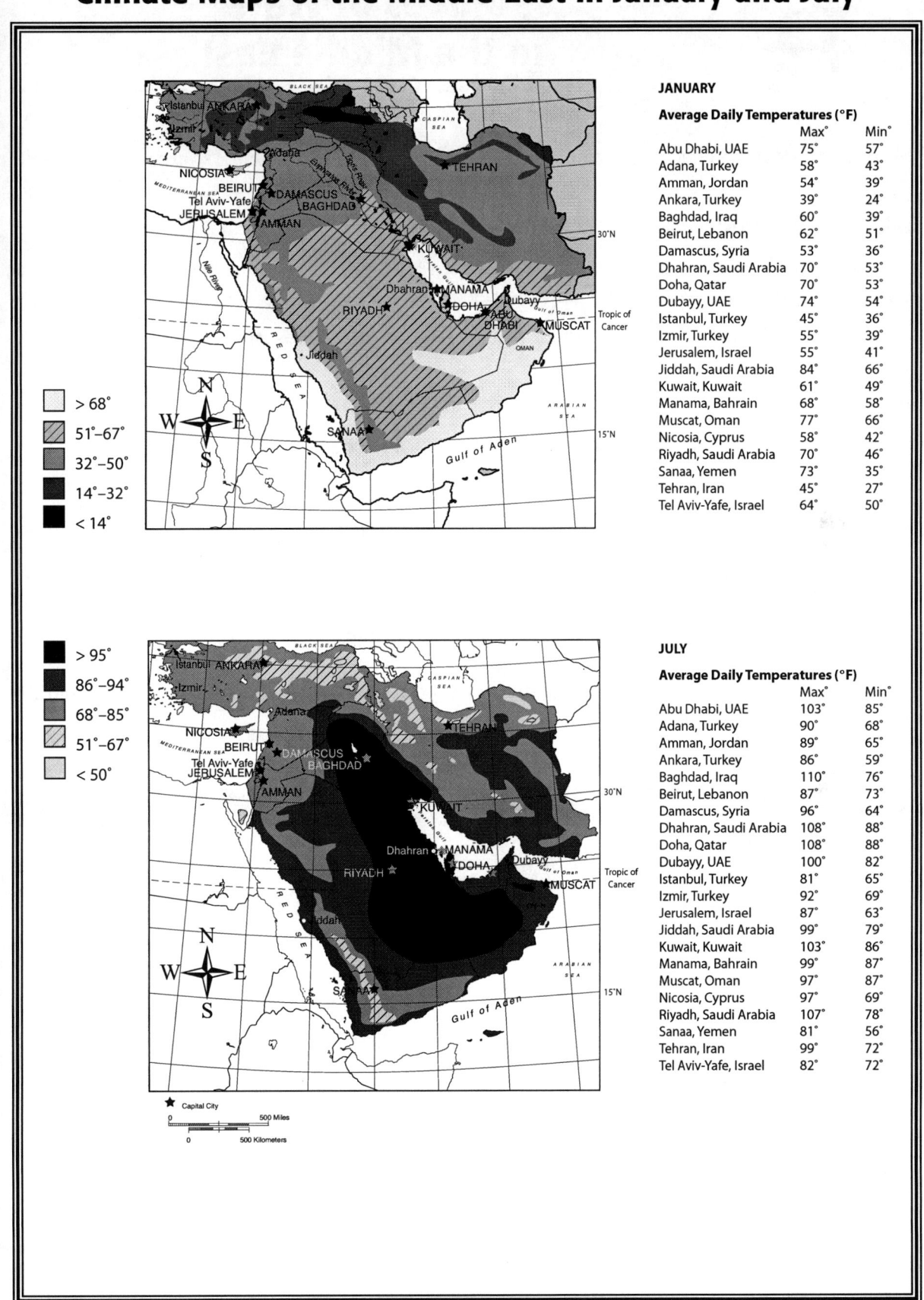

Legend (January map):
- > 68°
- 51°–67°
- 32°–50°
- 14°–32°
- < 14°

JANUARY
Average Daily Temperatures (°F)

	Max°	Min°
Abu Dhabi, UAE	75°	57°
Adana, Turkey	58°	43°
Amman, Jordan	54°	39°
Ankara, Turkey	39°	24°
Baghdad, Iraq	60°	39°
Beirut, Lebanon	62°	51°
Damascus, Syria	53°	36°
Dhahran, Saudi Arabia	70°	53°
Doha, Qatar	70°	53°
Dubayy, UAE	74°	54°
Istanbul, Turkey	45°	36°
Izmir, Turkey	55°	39°
Jerusalem, Israel	55°	41°
Jiddah, Saudi Arabia	84°	66°
Kuwait, Kuwait	61°	49°
Manama, Bahrain	68°	58°
Muscat, Oman	77°	66°
Nicosia, Cyprus	58°	42°
Riyadh, Saudi Arabia	70°	46°
Sanaa, Yemen	73°	35°
Tehran, Iran	45°	27°
Tel Aviv-Yafe, Israel	64°	50°

Legend (July map):
- > 95°
- 86°–94°
- 68°–85°
- 51°–67°
- < 50°

JULY
Average Daily Temperatures (°F)

	Max°	Min°
Abu Dhabi, UAE	103°	85°
Adana, Turkey	90°	68°
Amman, Jordan	89°	65°
Ankara, Turkey	86°	59°
Baghdad, Iraq	110°	76°
Beirut, Lebanon	87°	73°
Damascus, Syria	96°	64°
Dhahran, Saudi Arabia	108°	88°
Doha, Qatar	108°	88°
Dubayy, UAE	100°	82°
Istanbul, Turkey	81°	65°
Izmir, Turkey	92°	69°
Jerusalem, Israel	87°	63°
Jiddah, Saudi Arabia	99°	79°
Kuwait, Kuwait	103°	86°
Manama, Bahrain	99°	87°
Muscat, Oman	97°	87°
Nicosia, Cyprus	97°	69°
Riyadh, Saudi Arabia	107°	78°
Sanaa, Yemen	81°	56°
Tehran, Iran	99°	72°
Tel Aviv-Yafe, Israel	82°	72°

★ Capital City

LESSON 12

Sources of Water in the Middle East

Goal: To develop concepts and skills related to reading maps of water sources and precipitation

National Geography Standards

Standard 1. How to use maps and other geographic representations, tools, and technologies to acquire, process, and report information from a spatial perspective.

Standard 7. The physical processes that shape the patterns of Earth's surface.

Preparing Students for Instruction

Before starting this activity, review the following terms and concepts:

+ How to interpret the symbols of a map key
+ terms: aquifer, desalination, groundwater, precipitation

Map Overview

Most countries have a double source of water for drinking and growing crops: rainfall (and other forms of precipitation) and ground-based sources such as aquifers and lakes. In large portions of the Middle East, there is almost no rainfall, so people must depend entirely on freshwater in aquifers and freshwater bodies of water such as lakes and rivers.

Answer Key
1. 0 to 12 inches
2. Israel, Lebanon, and parts of Syria, Turkey, Iraq, and Iran, and a small part of Yemen
3. Kuwait, Qatar, Bahrain, United Arab Emirates, Saudi Arabia, Israel, and Jordan
4. The Red Sea and the Persian Gulf
5. They are located near the Mediterranean Sea.
6. Oman and Yemen; students should note that neither country has any desalination plants or dams. Also, Yemen has only four oases, while Oman has one.

Discussion Guide

To support students in reflecting on the activities and to gather some formative information about student learning, use the following prompts to facilitate a class discussion to "debrief" the map activities.

Prompts/Questions

1. Do you think those countries with a good supply of water would share some with countries that have few water sources? Why or why not?
2. Why don't more countries have desalination plants?

Suggested Appropriate Responses

1. Answers will vary. Students may say that it would be a friendly and neighborly thing to do. It would make for good international relations. Others may say that those countries with a good supply need all the water they have and probably do not have enough to share.
2. Answers will vary. Some students may feel that desalination plants are expensive and countries don't have enough money for them, or don't want to spend money on them. Others may state that the countries that don't have desalination plants have good aquifers, adequate rainfall, plus some rivers and lakes, so they don't need desalination plants.

Extending and Enhancing Learning

- Have students research water usage in a single Middle Eastern country. Where does the water come from? How is it distributed for use? Are larger populations clustered near areas with a plentiful water supply?
- For students who need more support, have them make a chart with each Middle Eastern country listed, and next to each country two columns, one showing the range of annual precipitation and the other showing other sources of water for each country.
- To challenge students further, have them research the process of desalination. When was it first thought of? When and where was the first plant constructed? How efficient is the process—i.e., how many gallons of sea water are needed to make one gallon of fresh water?

Name: _____

LESSON 12
Sources of Water in the Middle East

> **Geography Vocabulary**
>
> **aquifer:** an underground layer of earth, gravel, or porous stone that yields water
>
> **desalination:** the process of removing salt and other minerals from seawater to create freshwater
>
> **groundwater:** water beneath the earth's surface, often between saturated soil and rock, that supplies wells and springs
>
> **precipitation:** the falling of water in the form of rain, sleet, hail, or snow

✦ Reading the Maps

In most parts of the world, people receive the water they need from two sources: rainfall and ground-based sources of water. In much of the Middle East, there is hardly any rainfall. People must depend on springs, wells, rivers, and a process called "desalination" to get water. Desalination removes the salt from seawater and makes it suitable for use as freshwater. One map shows ground-based sources of water in the Middle East and the locations of desalination plants. The other map shows the "mean annual precipitation," which means average rainfall (plus other forms of water falling from the sky) in one year.

✦ Understanding the Maps

1. What is the mean annual precipitation for most of the Middle East?
2. Which areas in the Middle East receive 20 to 39 inches of rain per year?
3. Which countries have desalination plants?
4. From which two bodies of water do these countries obtain water that can be desalinated?

✦ Analyzing the Maps

5. Many of the areas in the Middle East that receive 20 to 39 inches of rain per year have a geographical feature in common. What is it?
6. Which two countries seem to have the fewest sources of water? Explain.

Name: _____

Mean Annual Precipitation in the Middle East

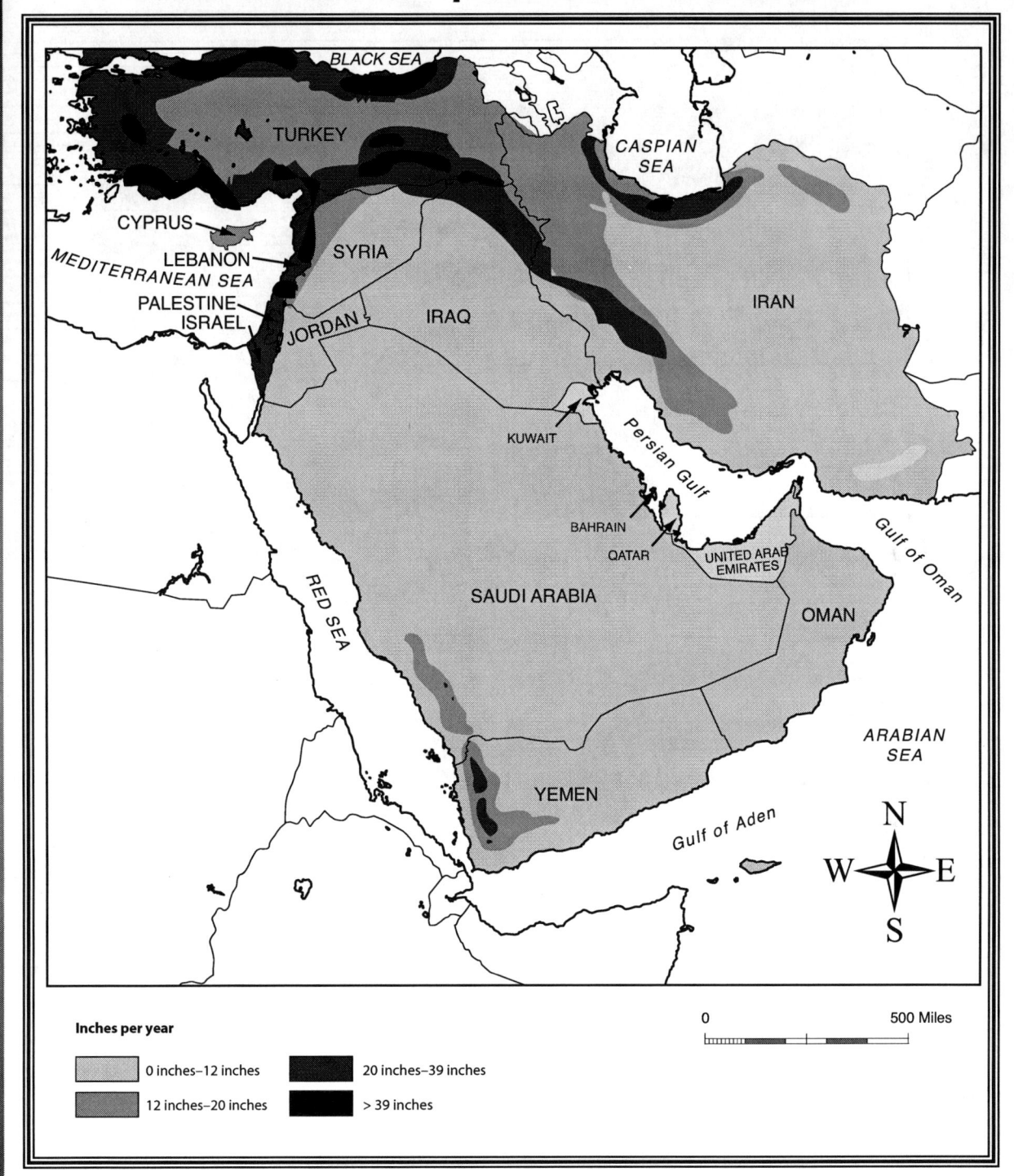

Inches per year

- 0 inches–12 inches
- 12 inches–20 inches
- 20 inches–39 inches
- > 39 inches

Name: _____

Sources of Water in the Middle East

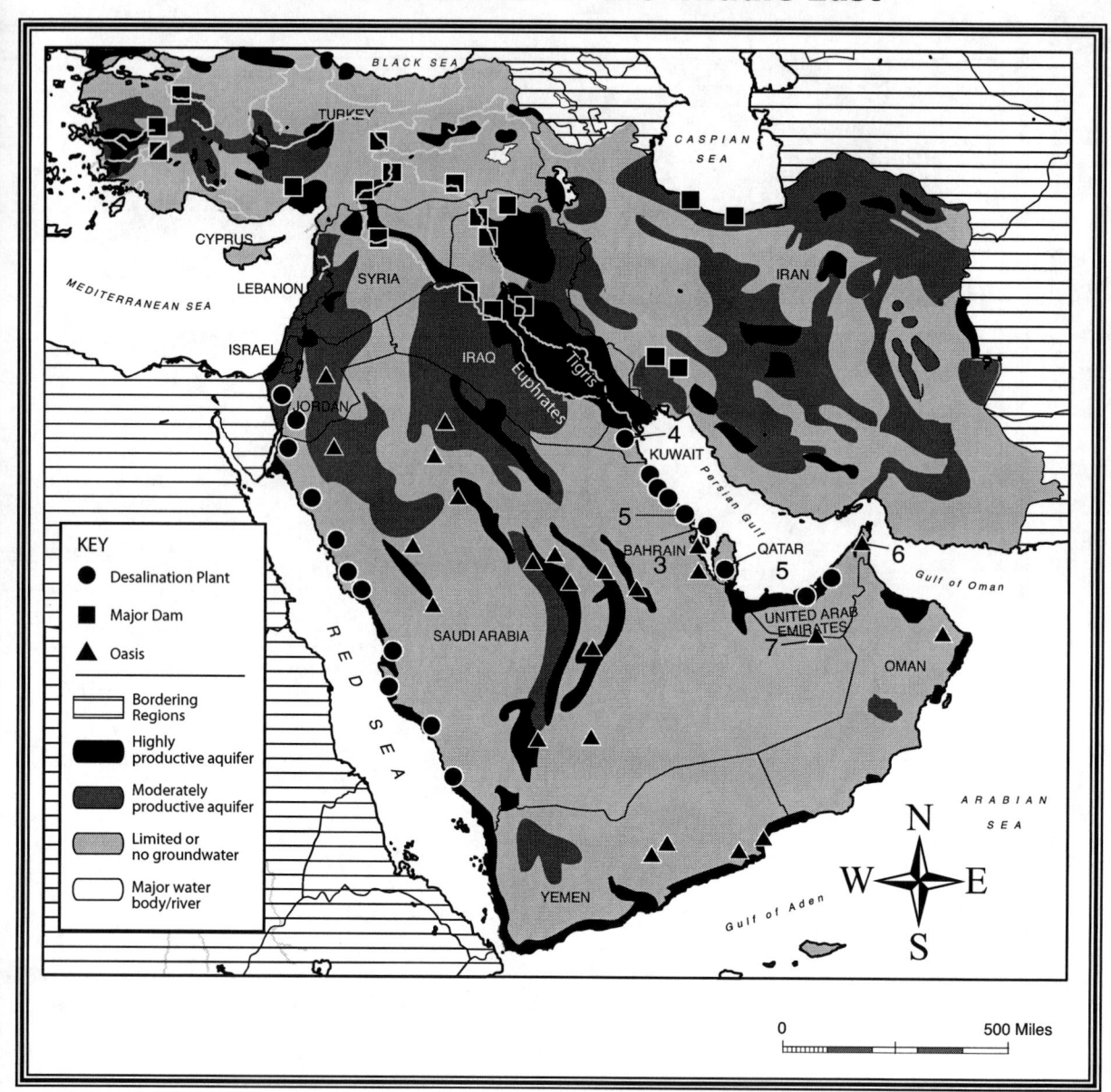

LESSON 13
Coral Reef Ecosystems of the Middle East

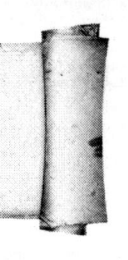

Goal: To develop concepts and skills related to understanding ecosystems based on coral reefs in the Middle East

National Geography Standards

Standard 1. How to use maps and other geographic representations, tools, and technologies to acquire, process, and report information from a spatial perspective.

Standard 9. The characteristics and spatial distribution of ecosystems on Earth's surface.

Preparing Students for Instruction

Before starting this activity, review the following information about ecosystems and coral reefs:

- An ecosystem is an interdependent group of living things occupying the same space. A common example is a grassland, where prairie dogs burrow under the grass for homes and feed on the grass for food. Hawks and wolves feed on the prairie dogs. If one aspect of an ecosystem is changed, all the living creatures are affected. For example, if the grass dried up in a drought, the prairie dogs would die of starvation and so would the predators that feed on them.

- In the case of coral reefs, the coral animals make the reefs feed on tiny organisms in the water where they are and also get some nourishment from sea grasses and mangroves along the banks. Presently the coral reefs of the Middle East are abundant because their habitat is relatively unaffected by pollution, although some oil pollution leaks into the waters. They thrive in areas with small human populations and no manufacturing to dump waste into the sea. Varieties of fish are dependent on coral reefs for shelter from predators and as sources of food.

Map Overview

This map shows the distribution of coral reefs in the waters of the Middle East in the late 1990s. As you can see, the entire Red Sea is lined with coral reefs, as is part of the Persian Gulf.

Answer Key
1. Saudi Arabia and Yemen
2. Persian Gulf
3. Gulf of Aden
4. Answers will vary but should include the following as possible reasons: too many humans or industries dumping waste in the water and polluting it so corals can't grow, or lack of sea grasses and mangroves that corals feed on. Note that there is shallow water near this coastline, so water depth is not the reason for a lack of coral reefs.
5. 200 meters or less
6. The water there is shallow, about 200 meters in depth.

© 2010 Walch Education

Discussion Guide

To support students in reflecting on the activities and to gather some formative information about student learning, use the following prompts to facilitate a class discussion to "debrief" the map activities.

Prompts/Questions

1. What do you think can be done to preserve these coral reefs from possible destruction?
2. How might the existence of coral reefs be an aid to ships navigating these waters?

Suggested Appropriate Responses

1. Answers may vary but might include that dumping of waste along those shores should be prohibited and growth of cities minimized. Mangroves and sea grasses should be encouraged to grow.
2. They would identify the locations of the most shallow water so ships could avoid being grounded.

Extending and Enhancing Learning

- Have students study other ecosystems in the Middle East, such as desert ecosystems in Arabia, and make a map showing the range of these ecosystems.

- For students who need more support, have them do Internet research on coral reefs. They should find out where else in the world coral reefs are located, what their sizes are, and whether any are endangered.

- To challenge students further, have them pick one form of animal life in the Middle East (for example, a camel) and research this animal's natural environment, its adaptation to that environment, what it eats and what predators eat it, and so on. Students then create a report that includes a map showing the dispersal of these animals and a drawing of the animal.

Name: _____

LESSON 13
Coral Reef Ecosystems of the Middle East

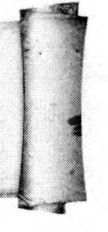

Geography Vocabulary

coral reefs: structures produced by living organisms, found in shallow, clear marine waters

ecosystem: a unit of interdependent organisms that share the same habitat

✦ Reading the Map

This map shows the distribution of coral reefs along the shores of two bodies of water in the Middle East. As you look at the map, note the areas where reefs are found and also note waters where there are no coral reefs.

✦ Understanding the Map

1. Coral reefs are located on the shores of the Red Sea near which two Middle Eastern countries?

2. Coral reefs near Kuwait and Qatar are located on what body of water?

3. What body of water on this map has almost no coral reefs, with just a small amount of reef in the western corner?

✦ Analyzing the Map

4. Why do you think that Yemen's border with the Gulf of Aden does not have any coral reefs?

5. What water depth seems to be just right for coral reefs?

6. On the lower right of your map, locate the colony of coral reefs that is not near any land. Why do you think that colony grew in that particular location? Explain.

© 2010 Walch Education   Critical Thinking About Geography: The Middle East   **59**

Name: _____

Coral Reef Ecosystems of Middle Eastern Waters

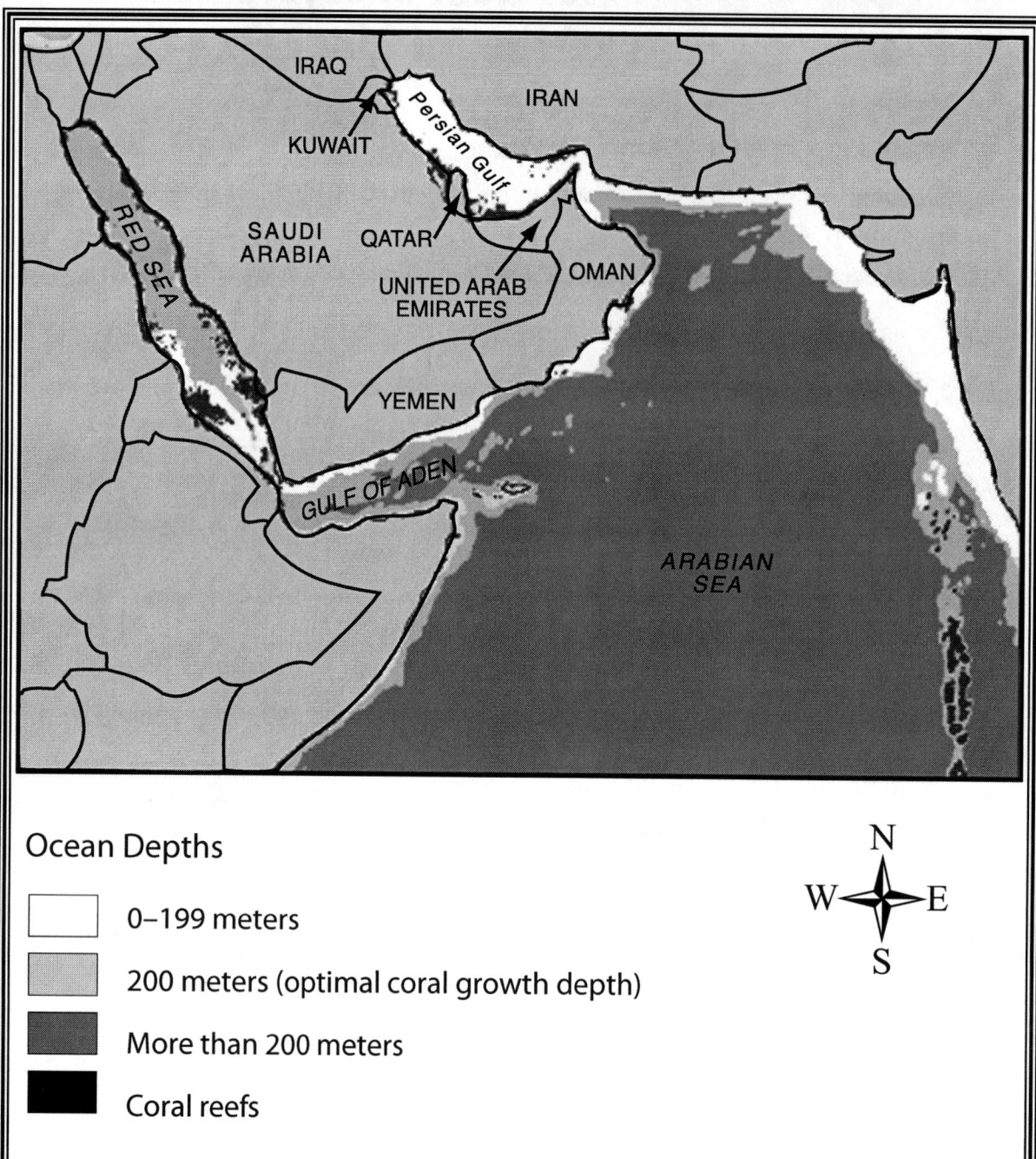

Ocean Depths

- ☐ 0–199 meters
- ▒ 200 meters (optimal coral growth depth)
- ▓ More than 200 meters
- ■ Coral reefs

60 Critical Thinking About Geography: The Middle East © 2010 Walch Education

LESSON 14
Comparing Historic and Modern Maps of the Middle East

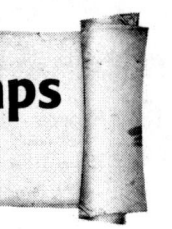

Goal: To develop concepts and skills related to making comparisons of historical and contemporary maps of the same area

National Geography Standards

Standard 1. How to use maps and other geographic representations, tools, and technologies to acquire, process, and report information from a spatial perspective.

Standard 3. How to analyze the spatial organization of people, places, and environments on Earth's surface.

Standard 13. How the forces of cooperation and conflict among people influence the division and control of Earth's surface.

Preparing Students for Instruction

Before starting this activity, review the following information with students:

- Over time, an area such as the Middle East will have changing national boundaries, depending on invasion from outside and inner conflicts that are resolved by division or joining of land areas. The area we call the Middle East today came under the control of an ever-changing array of conquerors, invaders, and rulers for thousands of years.

Map Overview

The first map shows the national boundaries of the Middle East and its national divisions in the year 1860. Compare it with the contemporary map to see the changes that have taken place.

Answer Key
1. Persia
2. Yes
3. Pakistan and Iran
4. Syria, Lebanon, Israel, Iraq, and Kuwait
5. Qatar, Bahrain, and United Arab Emirates
6. Countries that were part of Turkey: Syria, Lebanon, Israel, Iraq, and Kuwait—Arabic is the official language for each of these, except Israel, which has two official languages, Hebrew and Arabic. Countries that were part of Arabia: Saudi Arabia, United Arab Emirates, Bahrain, Qatar, Oman, and Yemen—Arabic is the official language for each of these.

Discussion Guide

To support students in reflecting on the activities and to gather some formative information about student learning, use the following prompts to facilitate a class discussion to "debrief" the map activities.

Prompts/Questions

1. There are more countries in the Middle East now than there were in 1860. Why do you think larger countries would divide into smaller areas?

2. In 1990, Iraq invaded Kuwait, trying to annex that country. The United States and other nations forced Iraq to give up the effort. Do you think the smaller countries in the Middle East today are strong enough to exist without being absorbed back into one of the large countries? Why or why not?

Suggested Appropriate Responses

1. Answers may vary. Students might say that the smaller areas would split away from the larger country because of religious or cultural differences.

2. Students may say that smaller countries are safe because of organizations such as the United Nations that will support them if they are attacked. On the other hand, students may say that these smaller countries are in danger because they don't have the military forces to defend themselves.

Extending and Enhancing Learning

+ Have students locate and study other historic maps of the Middle East, particularly during the periods of the Christian crusades and the era of Muslim efforts to control the territory. Students can work in groups to prepare a report on how national divisions were drawn in these eras, and why. A map of the assigned era can be part of each group's report to the class.

+ For students who need more support, have them write the five major areas of the Middle East in 1860 (Turkey, Persia, Beloochistan, Arabia, and Afghanistan) across the top of a paper, and under each area, list the Middle Eastern countries that occupy the same areas now.

+ To challenge students further, have them research different eras in the history of the Middle East such as the Christian Crusades, the Muslim invasions of the Middle East, the rule of the Ottoman Empire, and the control of the British and French in the 20th century.

Name: _____

LESSON 14
Comparing Historic and Modern Maps of the Middle East

✦ Reading the Maps

The map on the next page shows how the Middle East looked in the year 1860. Compare this map with the Political Map of the Middle East to see what has changed.

✦ Understanding the Maps

1. What was the name in 1860 of the country that is now Iran?
2. Did all of the seas in the Middle East have the same names in 1860 as they do now?
3. The country called Beloochistan is now part of which two modern countries?
4. Which countries of today were once parts of Turkey but now are independent countries?
5. Which three countries now bordering the Persian Gulf were parts of Arabia in 1860?

✦ Analyzing the Maps

6. Considering their former nationalities, which modern countries are likely to speak the same language? State your answer in terms of what these countries used to be (e.g., "Countries that in 1860 were part of . . .") and then name the modern countries.

© 2010 Walch Education   Critical Thinking About Geography: The Middle East   63

Name: _____

The Middle East in 1860

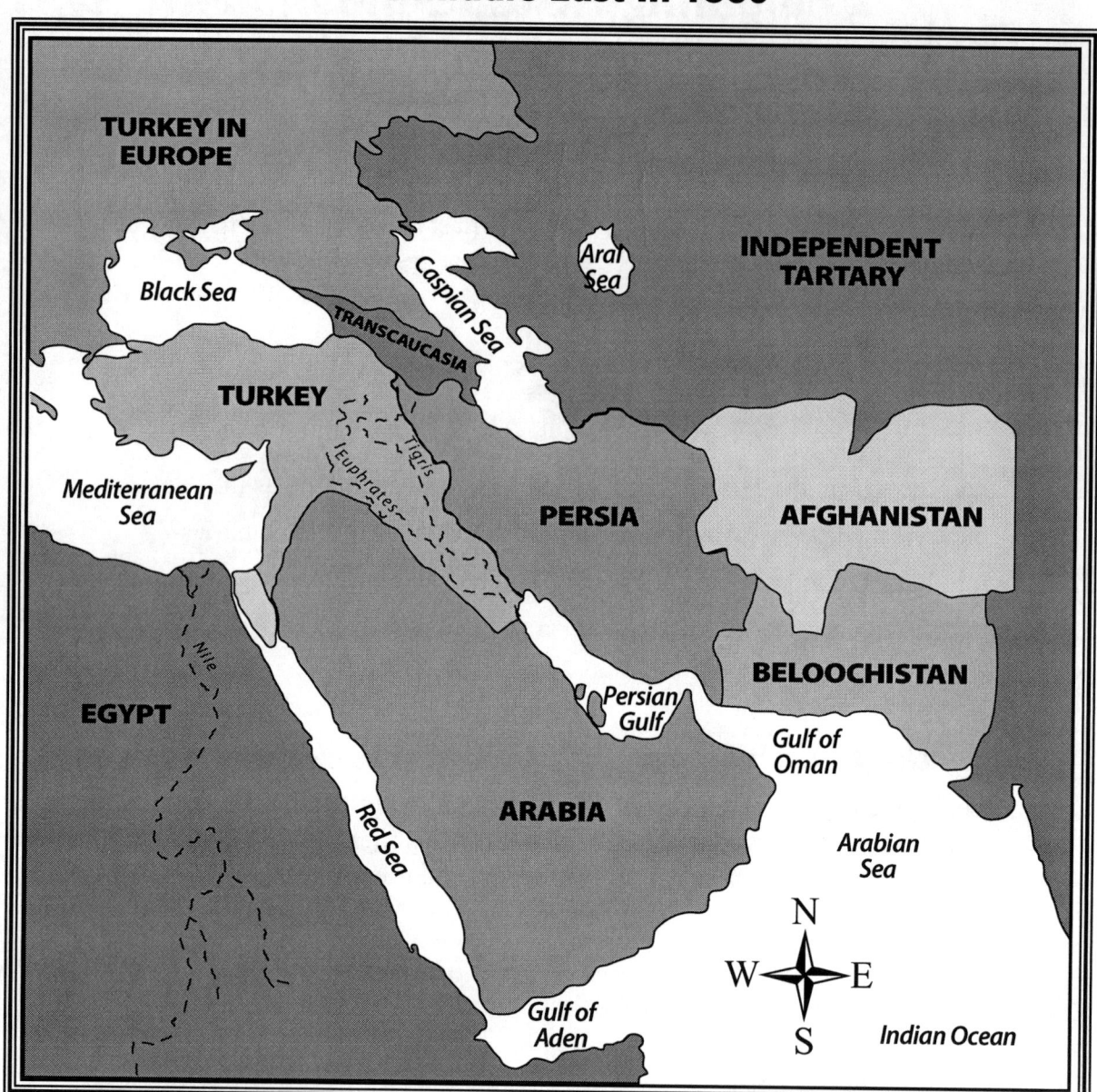

- TURKEY IN EUROPE
- Black Sea
- Aral Sea
- INDEPENDENT TARTARY
- Caspian Sea
- TRANSCAUCASIA
- TURKEY
- Tigris
- Euphrates
- Mediterranean Sea
- PERSIA
- AFGHANISTAN
- Nile
- BELOOCHISTAN
- EGYPT
- Persian Gulf
- Gulf of Oman
- Red Sea
- ARABIA
- Arabian Sea
- Gulf of Aden
- Indian Ocean

Name: _____

Political Map of the Middle East (Contemporary)

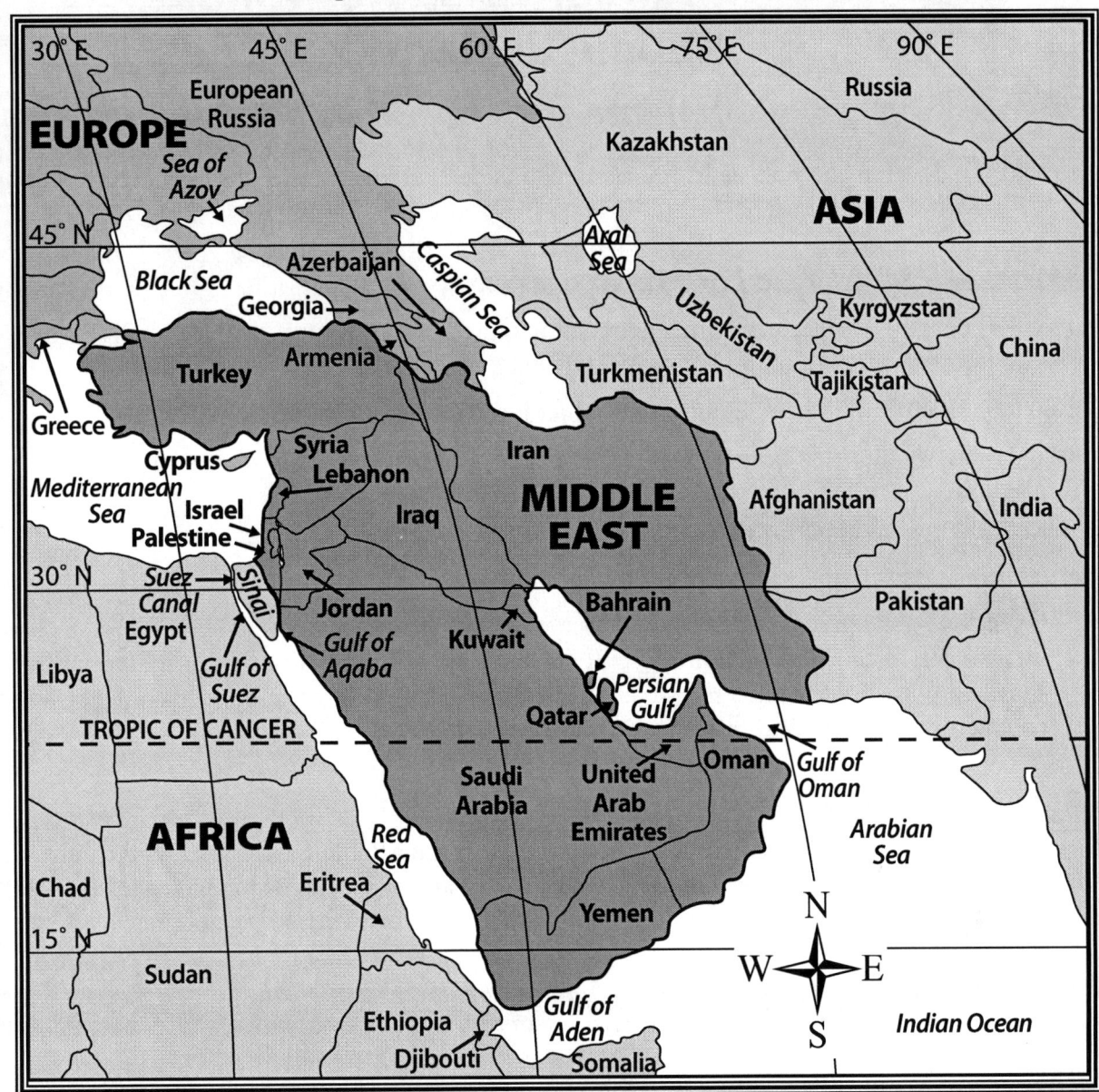

LESSON 15
Boundary Disputes Among Middle Eastern Countries

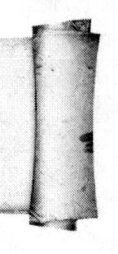

✦ **Goal:** To develop concepts and skills related to understanding that countries sometimes disagree on territorial borders

National Geography Standards

Standard 1. How to use maps and other geographic representations, tools, and technologies to acquire, process, and report information from a spatial perspective.

Standard 5. That people create regions to interpret Earth's complexity.

Standard 6. How culture and experience influence people's perceptions of places and regions.

Preparing Students for Instruction

Before starting this activity, review the following information with students:

✦ Over time, an area such as the Middle East will have changing national boundaries, depending on invasion from outside and inner conflicts that are resolved by division or joining of land areas. The area we call the Middle East today came under the control of an ever-changing array of conquerors, invaders, and rulers for thousands of years.

Map Overview

This map shows boundary disputes among the countries of the Middle East. Explain that many of the disputes are related either to oil resources or to access to waterways. Have students read each of the numbered markings that give details of the disputes and how they were or were not resolved.

Answer Key	
1.	The line indicates that this boundary is a politically tense frontier.
2.	Any three of the following: Iran's boundary with Turkmenistan, Afghanistan, and Pakistan; Saudi Arabia's boundary with UAE and Oman; Iraq's boundaries with Saudi Arabia and Jordan; Jordan's borders with Syria and Saudi Arabia; Oman's border with Yemen
3.	The boundary between Iraq and Iran is the longest. Students may offer differing predictions about this boundary dispute classified as "volatile." Some may suggest that war might break out. Others may say that an organization such as the United Nations will have to monitor this boundary.
4.	Bahrain and Qatar
5.	Iran and Iraq
6.	Dispute number 5 between Iraq and Kuwait was based on a historic claim. Student attitudes toward the historic claim justification may vary. Some will feel that a country should have all its historic territory. Others may feel that the passage of time changes attitudes toward boundaries.

Discussion Guide

To support students in reflecting on the activities and to gather some formative information about student learning, use the following prompts to facilitate a class discussion to "debrief" the map activities.

Prompts/Questions

1. In addition to water and oil resources, what are other reasons why a country might want to take land from another country?
2. One solution to a boundary dispute is to have an arbitrator, a neutral entity such as a U.N. representative, decide the dispute. Why might countries agree to this solution?

Suggested Appropriate Responses

1. Answers will vary. Students may reason that some countries may want to increase their territory and thereby increase their wealth. Others may suggest that people of one religion may want to seize land belonging to people of another religion, possibly to convert them. Another possibility is so that people of one ethnic background can all be citizens of the same country. Still another is that historically the disputed territory may have belonged to one country but now is considered as part of another.
2. The alternative might be war. Also, countries would trust someone neutral more than they trust each other to solve the problem.

Extending and Enhancing Learning

+ Have students research boundary disputes in other parts of the world. For example, the United States and Great Britain had a serious dispute over the boundary between Washington state and Canada. How was that dispute resolved? What other boundary disputes existed in the United States? Students might also want to look into the historic dispute between China and Taiwan.

+ For students who need more support, have them list boundary disputes that have occurred in their own lives. For example, in a game, boundaries determine whether a ball is "in" or "out." Do boundaries exist at home? Perhaps students who share a room with a sibling divide the space into "mine" and "his." Fences around an area create boundaries. Are these a good idea? Why or why not? Do neighbors argue over boundaries, perhaps when a tree from one yard encroaches on another, or one neighbor builds a fence on property claimed by the other neighbor? How are these disputes resolved? Have students work in pairs to list as many "real-life" boundary disputes as they can, and actual or potential solutions.

+ To challenge students further, have them work in teams to research more deeply the Middle Eastern boundary disputes depicted on this map. Assign each team a different disputed territory. Have teams report on the history of the dispute and the reasons behind it, and then predict how it might be decided in the future. Students should include a map of that area in their report.

Name: _____

LESSON 15
Boundary Disputes Among Middle Eastern Countries

> **Geography Vocabulary**
>
> **national boundaries:** lines marking limits between countries
>
> **territory:** a defined area, including land and water, owned by a country

✦ Reading the Map

Often countries do not agree on where one country ends and the other begins. Boundary disputes can lead to invasions of territory and even to war. In the Middle East, the boundary disputes shown on your map seem to have been caused by a variety of reasons. Read the numbered explanations as you look at the map. Analyze the reasons for these disputes.

✦ Understanding the Map

Look at the lines as they are shown on the map, and consult the map key to find the answers to questions 1 through 3.

1. What type of boundary is between Saudi Arabia and Yemen?

2. Name three countries that have a calm frontier.

3. Where is the longest boundary that is classified as Volatile Frontier? "Volatile" means "tending to erupt in violence." What do you think may happen to this frontier?

✦ Analyzing the Map

4. Which countries are involved in a dispute that seems to be caused by both countries wanting the same piece of land because it may contain oil resources?

5. Which boundary dispute involves access to a waterway?

6. Which boundary dispute was based on a historic claim to the disputed territory? Do you think this is a good reason for a country to seize territory? Why?

68 Critical Thinking About Geography: The Middle East   © 2010 Walch Education

Name: _____

Boundary Disputes in the Middle East

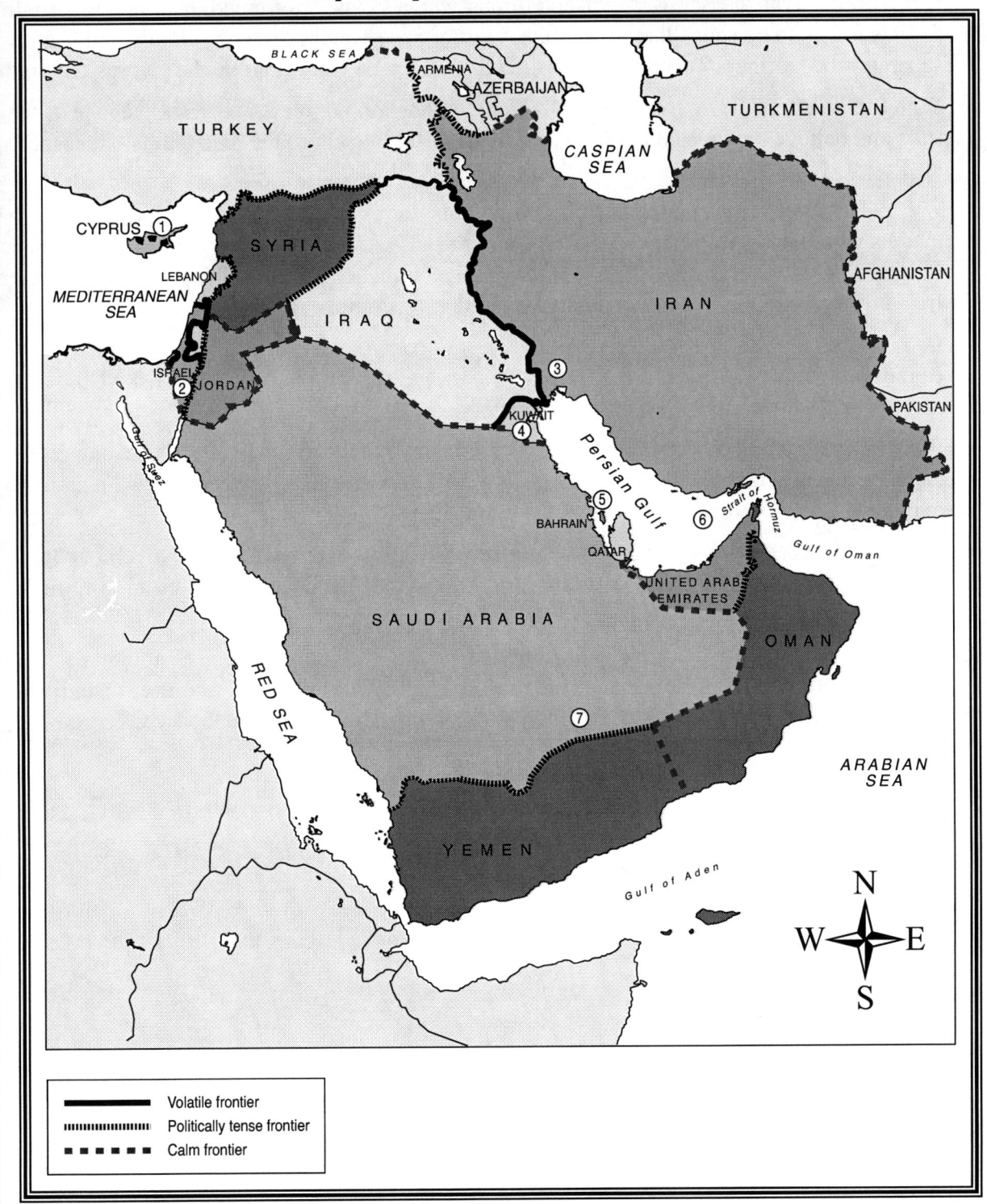

Volatile frontier
Politically tense frontier
Calm frontier

(continued)

Name: _____

1. In 1974, the Greek government sponsored a sudden change in government in Cyprus. Right after that, Turkey invaded Cyprus. At the end of that war, a treaty determined that the northern third of the island would be controlled by Turkey. A buffer zone watched over by the United Nations now separates the Northern Turkish Cypriot area from the area controlled by the Cyprus government.

2. With the exception of Egypt, Israel's Arabic neighbors do not recognize the existence of the Jewish state and believe the Palestinian Arabs are the rightful owners of the land that is Israeli-occupied territory.

3. The 1975 Algiers accord moved the Iraq–Iran boundaries in the Shatt Al waterway so that both nations would have access to the sea via the waterway. After the start of the Iran–Iraq War in 1980, Iraq refused to honor the accord and reasserted its boundary claims to the low-water mark on the Iranian shoreline. The border is officially closed at this time.

4. Iraq invaded Kuwait in 1990. Iraq claimed Kuwait based on pre-World War I boundaries. U.S.-led coalition forces drove Iraqi forces from Kuwait in February 1991. Iraq accepted a U.N. resolution that restored Kuwait to its pre-invasion territory.

5. Bahrain was granted ownership of the Hawar Islands by the British in 1939. The islands, which are actually closer to Qatar, may have oil, and are currently disputed between the two nations. Bahrain maintains a small military garrison on the main island.

6. Iran occupied the islands of Abu Musa and Tun As Sigrah Tun al Kubra on November 30, 1971, one day before the British were to transfer control of the islands to the United Arab Emirates. Currently the UAE claims the land, which remains occupied by Iran.

7. The 1955 Modified Riyadh Line defined by the British is commonly used as a line of reference between eastern Saudi Arabia and its neighbors. The line was intended to prevent Saudi Arabia from taking Rhub Al Khali. In 1974, a Saudi–United Arab Emirates boundary was established, but the UAE has yet to ratify that agreement.

Glossary

aquifer: an underground layer of earth, gravel, or porous stone that yields water

arable: fit for growing crops

average daily temperature: the average of the high and low temperatures for a given day

average maximum temperature: the average of the high temperatures for a given period

average minimum temperature: the average of low temperatures for a given period

average monthly temperature: the average of the "average daily temperatures" for a given month

barrels per day: a unit measuring the rate at which petroleum is produced at the refinery

basin: a large, bowl-shaped depression in the surface of the land or ocean floor

compass rose: an element of a map used to show direction

continents: the major land masses on earth

coral reefs: structures produced by living organisms, found in shallow, clear marine waters

desalination: the process of removing salt and other minerals from seawater to create freshwater

distortion: a change in the shape of an image resulting from imperfections in portraying it

ecosystem: a group of interdependent organisms that share the same habitat

equator: a line of latitude that circles the earth and divides it evenly in half

expressway: a major divided highway with few intersections

groundwater: water beneath the earth's surface, often between saturated soil and rock, that supplies wells and springs

gulf: a large area of a sea or ocean partially enclosed by land

industry: the production and sale of goods

irrigated farming: bringing water to otherwise dry land in order to plant crops there

latitude: imaginary circles on the earth's surface, parallel to the equator and above and below it

longitude: imaginary lines on the earth's surface passing through the North and South poles

map projections: attempts to portray the surface of the earth or a portion of the earth on a flat surface

meridian: a line of longitude; an imaginary great circle on the earth's surface passing through the North and South poles

national boundaries: lines marking limits between countries

natural resources: material occurring in nature, such as coal, oil, and minerals, that can be used to create wealth

Nomadic: referring to a group of people who move from place to place with flocks of animals seeking grass for grazing

oasis: a place with a water source in an otherwise dry area

parallels: lines of latitude; imaginary circles on the earth's surface, parallel to the equator and above and below it

petroleum: a flammable liquid occurring naturally in deposits under the earth's surface, used to manufacture gasoline and other products

physical map: a map that indicates the location of landforms, such as deserts, mountains, plains, and rivers

political map: a map showing countries in a region, or a single country's territories, states or provinces, boundaries, and capitals

population density: the number of people living in a given amount of space

precipitation: the falling of water in the form of rain, sleet, hail, or snow

prime meridian: the line of longitude numbered zero

site map: a detailed map of a relatively small area

territory: a defined area, including land and water, owned by a country

Tropic of Cancer: a line of latitude about 23 degrees north of the equator

Tropic of Capricorn: a line of latitude about 23 degrees south of the equator

WALCH EDUCATION
extending and enhancing learning

Let's stay in touch!

Thank you for purchasing these Walch Education materials. Now, we'd like to support you in your role as an educator. **Register now** and we'll provide you with updates on related publications, online resources, and more. You can register online at www.walch.com/newsletter, or fill out this form and fax or mail it to us.

Name _____ Date _____

School name _____

School address _____

City _____ State _____ Zip _____

Phone number (home) _____ (school) _____

E-mail _____

Grade level(s) taught _____ Subject area(s) _____

Where did you purchase this publication? _____

When do you primarily purchase supplemental materials? _____

What moneys were used to purchase this publication?

    [ ] School supplemental budget

    [ ] Federal/state funding

    [ ] Personal

    [ ] Please sign me up for Walch Education's free quarterly e-newsletter, *Education Connection.*

    [ ] Please notify me regarding free *Teachable Moments* downloads.

    [ ] Yes, you may use my comments in upcoming communications.

COMMENTS _____

_____

_____

_____

Please FAX this completed form to 888-991-5755, or mail it to:
Customer Service, Walch Education, 40 Walch Drive, Portland, ME 04103